ABOUT THE AUTHOR

Yasser Usman is a television journalist and India's most loved film biographer. He has bagged the prestigious Ramnath Goenka Award for Excellence in Journalism. He has also been a recipient of the NT (News Television) Awards three years in a row. He is the author of the bestselling books — *Rajesh Khanna: The Untold Story of India's First Superstar*, *Rekha: The Untold Story* and *Sanjay Dutt: The Crazy Untold Story of Bollywood's Bad Boy*. This is his fourth book.

Praise for *Rajesh Khanna: The Untold Story of India's First Superstar*

'The book packs a punch while constructing the story of the biggest star of Hindi cinema.' —***India Today***

'As you read this book you will smile at some places, your eyes will be moist at others…an experience similar to watching a Rajesh Khanna blockbuster.' —**Salim Khan (Veteran screenwriter)**

Praise for *Rekha: The Untold Story*

'Yasser Usman takes a close look at the actress' life but remains sympathetic' —***Hindustan Times***

'*Rekha: The Untold Story* by Yasser Usman exposes a dark side of Bollywood. The book tells how Rekha overcame several odds to become one of the greatest actresses of Indian cinema… This assessment, and accusations of misogyny, will be an eye-opener for those who see Bollywood as trendy and cool.' —***The National*, UAE**

'Document[s]…the phenomenal rise of the underdog in an overtly patriarchal industry' —***Vogue***

'A riveting book' —***The Mint***

'A racy read' —***The Asian Age***

'[Has] to be read to be believed' —***India Today***

'Reveals shocking details' —***DNA***

'An eye-opener' —***The News Minute***

'Crisp, well-paced' —***Firstpost***

'It is difficult to be unmoved by Rekha's story' —***Hindustan Times***

'[Usman] has an eye for human drama…we are constantly intrigued by and care about [Rekha's] story…[Also] He shows empathy, something Rekha has been denied for long.' —***OPEN Magazine***

'…it is a compulsive read and will keep you thoroughly engaged.' —***Dawn***

Praise for *Sanjay Dutt: The Crazy Untold Story of Bollywood's Bad Boy*

'A "film-like" narrative…poignant…thorough.' —***Business Standard***

'This isn't fanboy writing… lets the ugly speaks for itself.' —***Mint***

GURU DUTT

An Unfinished Story

YASSER USMAN

SIMON & SCHUSTER

London · New York · Sydney · Toronto · New Delhi

First published in India by Simon & Schuster India, 2020
A VIACOMCBS Company

Copyright © Yasser Usman, 2020

The right of Yasser Usman to be identified as author of this work has been asserted by him in accordance with Section 57 of the Copyright Act, 1957.

1 3 5 7 9 10 8 6 4 2

Simon & Schuster India
818, Indraprakash Building,
21, Barakhamba Road,
New Delhi 110001

www.simonandschuster.co.in

Paperback: 978-93-92099-08-3
eBook: 978-93-86797-89-6

The views and opinions expressed in this work are the author's own and the facts are as reported by him, and the publisher is in no way liable for the same.

Typeset in India by SÜRYA, New Delhi
Printed and bound in India by Replika Press Pvt. Ltd.

Simon & Schuster India is committed to sourcing paper that is made from wood grown in sustainable forests and support the Forest Stewardship Council, the leading international forest certification organisation. Our books displaying the FSC logo are printed on FSC certified paper.

No part of this publication may be reproduced, transmitted or stored in a retrieval system, in any form or by any means, electronic, mechanical, photocopying, recording or otherwise, without the prior permission of the publisher.

This book is sold subject to the condition that it shall not, by way of trade or otherwise, be lent, resold, hired out, or otherwise circulated, without the publisher's prior consent, in any form of binding or cover other than that in which it is published.

To

Lalitha Lajmi, eminent artist and Guru Dutt's sister

With heartfelt gratitude,
Thank you for sharing your memories of the life and times of Guru and Geeta Dutt

CONTENTS

SECTION FOUR: DESTRUCTION OF A DREAM

SECTION FIVE: BUILDING OF A DREAM

SECTION SIX: DESTRUCTION OF A DREAM

SECTION SEVEN: BUILDING OF A DREAM

SECTION TWELVE: DESTRUCTION OF A DREAM

SECTION THIRTEEN: BUILDING OF A DREAM

SECTION FOURTEEN: DESTRUCTION OF A DREAM

SECTION FIFTEEN: 1964

PROLOGUE

BERLIN, 1963

Sahib Bibi aur Ghulam was India's official entry at the 13th Berlin International Film Festival. On 26 June 1963, its lead actors, Guru Dutt and Waheeda Rehman, attended the festival along with the film's director, Abrar Alvi. The screening took place the next day but the film failed to create any flutter as the international audience could not relate to the overt melodrama and the very Indian theme. This, despite the fact that the film had been trimmed specially for the festival. There were hardly twenty-five people in the theatre and their interest in the film could not be sustained. The film was outrightly rejected.

Guru Dutt walked out of his own screening.

On this very same trip, Waheeda Rehman—Guru Dutt's protégé, and the one and only lead actress in his films for a substantial part of his career—conclusively yet gracefully conveyed the end of her relationship with Guru Dutt.

'Yes. The last time I saw him must have been in Berlin,' said Waheeda Rehman.[1] Things had started to unravel towards the close of their last shoot together for *Sahib Bibi Aur Ghulam*. Guru Dutt's younger sister, the eminent artist Lalitha Lajmi, remembers, 'Waheeda and Guru Dutt had almost parted. She used to invite us both sometimes for dinner and my brother knew she was friendly with me. l heard Guru Dutt went with a bouquet of flowers to her home and the doors were not opened to him. Perhaps it was after this incident l had visited him and for the first time he told me not to keep in touch with her any more.'

The very next day, Guru Dutt left Berlin.

Legendary film maker B.R. Chopra recalled,[2] 'That man, Guru Dutt, drank all the way back from Berlin to Bombay while keeping all to himself in a corner seat. We knew all about Waheeda having told him, point-blank that she had made up her mind about him and that was it. She also discreetly left Guru Dutt to find his own way back. Guru Dutt was clearly heading towards turning into a mental and physical wreck…I instinctively knew that it was the beginning of the end.'

Guru Dutt used up all the sleeping pills that he had carried with him to Berlin. He didn't sleep for the next four nights. 'He said to me, "I think I will go mad"', recalled Bimal Mitra, the writer of *Sahib, Biwi aur Ghulam* and undoubtedly a giant in the literary world from Bengal.

Bombay, 1963

Back in Bombay, his wife Geeta Dutt—the glorious singer who had broken playback singing traditions to bring a fresh naturalness to Indian film songs—had started blaming their bungalow for all their woes. They shared only a decade old but widely celebrated story—the star singer and the struggling film-maker having found love in tinseltown. Deep down she believed that their relationship had developed an irreparable rift only after they shifted to this bungalow in the very posh locality of Pali Hill.

Lalitha Lajmi, who witnessed the relationship from the early days of courtship till the end, further recalls,[3] 'She believed that the bungalow was haunted. There was a particular tree in the house and she said there's a ghost who lives in that tree, who is bringing bad omen and ruining their marriage. She also had something against a Buddha statue that was kept in their huge drawing room.' According to Lalitha, it was Geeta who had suggested that they must leave.

This prospect was heartbreaking for Guru Dutt.

It had been his dream house—but never the home he had always longed for.

Guru Dutt had twice attempted to kill himself in this house and survived both attempts.

Once, after surviving a suicide attempt, a close friend asked Guru Dutt,[4] 'Why should you have done it? You have fame, you have wealth, you have the adoration of the masses. You possess all that most people crave for! Why are you so dissatisfied with life?'

Guru Dutt replied, 'I am not dissatisfied with life, I am dissatisfied within myself. True, I have all that people crave for. Still I don't have that which most people possess—a nook where one can repair [retire] to after the day's task is done, where one can find some peace and forget one's cares. If only I could get that, life would be worth living!'

From a house that had been home to the birth of so many great stories on celluloid, it now only birthed insomnia for Guru Dutt. So despite living in one of the most beautiful bungalows in Bombay's prime real estate, Guru Dutt would leave the house early every morning and reach his studio with sleep-deprived eyes. The studio wouldn't be open at that hour and silence hung all around it. Guru Dutt's man Friday, Ratan, would open the lock of the small chamber—a seven feet by seven feet room with a precious small bed. This is where Guru Dutt would lie down quietly and finally find sleep.

'I always wanted to be happy in my household. My house is the most beautiful among all the buildings in Pali Hill. Sitting in that house, it does not look like you are in Bombay. That garden, that ambience—where else can I find it? Despite this, I could not stay in that house for much longer,' once shared Guru Dutt.

Away from his luxurious and palatial bungalow, this small room was where he would find peace and sleep.

And then, on the morning of his birthday—ten days after his return from Berlin—he called in workers and told them to demolish his Pali Hill bungalow.

'I remember it was his birthday. He loved that house

and he was heartbroken when it was demolished,' recalls his sister Lalitha Lajmi.

The next time writer Bimal Mitra came to Bombay, he was taken to a new flat where Guru Dutt was living on rent. He was surprised and asked Guru what happened to the bungalow. Guru didn't reply.

Mitra recalled, 'In the car I asked him, "Why did you break that house?"'

Guru seemed shocked at this direct question. He said, 'Would you like to go there, to see that house?'

'Let's go,' said Mitra.

Guru turned the car around.

'We had descended down the steep slope of Pali Hill. We went back towards his bungalow. Taking several turns, our car reached the bungalow.'

The same bungalow number 48 of Pali Hill.

But everything looked different now. Guru Dutt's old concierge, Lala, was standing in front of the property. Bimal Mitra was stunned. The majestic bungalow where he had been a guest during his multiple script writing visits to Bombay had been razed to the ground. The room where Guru used to sleep now just had rubble in its place. Broken Italian blue marble was lying in place of the exquisite bathroom.

All he could see was splintered timber, chunks of plaster and shattered pieces of a dream.

He looked at Guru Dutt who was silently staring into space, lost in his thoughts. Mitra couldn't gather the courage to say anything. They walked in silence back to the car when Mitra asked him, 'But what is the real reason for demolishing the bungalow? That bungalow was...?'

'Because of Geeta,' Guru said in a low voice.

'What does that even mean?' Mitra asked

Guru took a puff of his cigarette, and gently explained, '*Ghar na hone ki takleef se, ghar hone ki takleef aur bhayankar hoti hai.*'[5]

It seems like sharp reminder of the scene from their film *Sahib Bibi Aur Ghulam* where Guru Dutt, playing a middle-aged architect, goes back to the haveli and asks the workers to pull it down. His life and cinema kept merging with each other like that.

About a year later, the last shot he gave was for the film *Baharen Phir Bhi Aayengi*. Playing a reporter, he hands over his resignation letter to his editor and says, 'I am leaving.'

Bombay, 1964

Geeta Dutt was really restless that night after another argument with Guru Dutt. She had shifted to her mother's house leaving Guru alone, who was staying at the rented Pedder Road apartment.

She had a strange premonition. In the early hours of the next morning she called up the house and asked the servant to check on Guru. The servant informed her that the door was locked from inside. Geeta asked the servant to break open the door.

It was 10.30 AM on 10 October 1964. A Saturday.

'I have such vivid memory of his death. I remember his right arm was stretched out, his eyes half-open as if he was about to get up, about to say something,' recalls Lalitha, his sister.

Wearing a kurta-pyjama, sprawled on his back, eyes closed, face inclined to the right and relaxed in a serene repose.

On the side table was a glass filled with a pink liquid—sleeping pills crushed and dissolved in water. There was an unfinished Hindi novel by his side and the lights were on. It looked like a thought-out scene straight out of one of his films. He had woven many spells through the poetic glances of his camera, the rhythm in his song sequences and the rebellion in his cinematic language. This was Guru Dutt's last spell. An unusual frame composition for his real death sequence.

Finally, his melancholy was over.

'When I met Geeta her first words to me were, "Lalli! I know all of you will blame me for his death,"' remembers Lalitha.

Guru Dutt died at the age of thirty-nine leaving behind a revered legacy in the short span of his career. A man of few words, who came to be celebrated for his brilliance only decades after his death.

Like his films, his life was a dream in two parts—the building of the dream and then the destruction of the dream.

We tell it here as it was.

Section One

THE BUILDING OF A DREAM

1925–30: MANGALORE TO CALCUTTA

'He was obsessed with shadow plays.'

1

THE BEGINNING

'Bring up your child in a good way, so that he would have the courage and character to face life.'

—Mohandas Karamchand Gandhi

Guru Dutt's mother Vasanthi and father Shivshankar Rao Padukone belonged to Mangalore's Saraswat community. The Konkani-speaking Saraswat community of Mangalore boasts of many scholars and artists. Shivshankar Padukone was from a modest background. He was pursuing a B.A. degree and was all of twenty years of age when he married the twelve-year-old Vasanthi in 1920. When Vasanthi reached puberty, the nuptial ceremony was performed. Vasanthi loved going to school but had to quit studies against her wishes.

Shivshankar was often unwell and was advised to see an astrologer. With Vasanthi, he went to meet the man, who also studied Vasanthi's palm. 'The astrologer gave me a broad smile when he examined my palm. He predicted that I would get a son within a year. He would be a good person and bring good luck to the family. The child would be world famous. I felt shy at that time; getting children at such a young age was unthinkable, recalled Vasanthi.'[6]

In 1924, the couple moved to Pannambur near Bangalore where Shivshankar Rao Padukone worked as a school headmaster. Mr Padukone was a man with a literary bent of mind and wrote poems in English, a language in which he was proficient. His dream was to write and edit journals. In his personal life, he was aloof, mostly lost in his dreams. He kept silent and there was little communication between him and his very young wife. Vasanthi wanted to learn the English language from her husband. 'I was longing to learn English. I did translations or made sentences in English, and he would correct them if he was in proper mood. But these occasions were rare. His short temper confused me, and I would stop learning.'

Shivshankar and Vasanthi were not happy together. The social norms in that day and age ruled that if you were married then had to 'learn to tolerate each other'. Vasanthi followed it too.

On 9 July 1925, exactly at noon, Vasanthi and Shivshankar's first child, Gurudutt Padukone, was born.

On the twelfth day, the cradle ceremony was performed and two names were suggested for the baby: Vasant Kumar and Gurudutt. The baby was born on a Thursday (Guruvaar) and it was also the birthday of Madhavacharya, the great philosopher and saint of the Vaishnava cult. So Gurudutt it was.[7]

Vasanthi's world now revolved around her first-born son and her mother came to live with them. The communication between Vasanthi and Shivshankar kept dwindling with time. She recounted, 'I was not close to my husband. We were poles apart. The wife had neither choice nor voice in any matters. Women had only to be submissive and obey their masters.'

Shivshankar resigned from his job as the school headmaster and shifted to Bangalore for a new job in a bank. But in his heart he wanted to pursue creative writing. Dissatisfied with the lack of creativity in his life and work, very soon Shivshankar resigned from his bank job too and moved to Mangalore. In Mangalore, he joined a printing press that published a weekly magazine. But he couldn't stay there for long either. Vasanthi was pregnant with her second child when Shivshankar resigned from the printing press too. The constant pressures of life were making him bitter.

During that phase of her life, Vasanthi had become so restless that she wanted to escape. In 1927, Mahatma Gandhi visited Bangalore. Vasanthi attended his prayer meetings and felt so peaceful that she wrote a letter to him describing her life and asking Gandhi ji to let her join the Sabarmati Ashram. Mahatma Gandhi wrote back.[8]

> Dear Vasanthi Devi,
>
> Recieved your letter. It was God's wish. You ought to stay where you are. Duty of a mother and wife is most important. Bring up your child in a good way, so that he would have the courage and character to face life. Serve our Bharatmata. Never give up hope.
>
> Ever yours
> Mohandas K. Gandhi

Perhaps Vasanthi followed Mahatma Gandhi's advice. Guru Dutt became the centre of her universe. The family went through severe financial struggles and lived in Bombay and Ahmedabad for short periods. But fate had its own way. Shivshankar never liked the city of Calcutta but got the job of a salesman in Calcutta.

The family then moved to Calcutta thinking that soon he would lose his job and they would have to go to a new city again. But later, Shivshankar found a job as an administrative clerk at the Burmah Shell Company. This was a job that finally gave the family the economic stability they were looking for. He went on to work with the company for the next thirty years.

Calcutta then became the city where Guru Dutt spent the formative years of his life. It became 'his city'. A culturally vibrant city that homed into his heart and mind and shaped the man he was to be.

2

A DISTURBED CHILDHOOD

CALCUTTA, 1929

> 'We had a disturbed childhood...our father did not believe in success. He believed in poetry which is not enough to survive. We looked upto our elder brother Guru Dutt.'
>
> —Lalitha Lajmi

Guru was four years old when his mother gave birth to her second son. He was named Shashidhar. Little Guru loved his kid brother but Shashidhar passed away due to illness when he was seven months old. He had severe convulsions. His brother's death traumatised Guru Dutt severely. Too young to understand death, Guru remained unwell for many weeks. For years after that Guru would remember him and weep.

The family lived in rented houses and changed many houses in Calcutta. Given the meagre income, there was hardly a concept of a stable home. Vasanthi had a third son

Atmaram, followed by their only daughter Lalitha. Lalitha was seven years younger to Guru Dutt. She later had two more sons, Devidutt and Vijay. Guru Dutt's sister, Lalitha Lajmi recounts, 'Financially, it was a difficult life. We lived in a tiny two-bedroom flat in Calcutta. There were our parents, my maternal grandmother and five of us kids. The flat was so small that we kept colliding into one another. Father was always lost in his own world. My grandmother ruled the household. She cooked, cleaned and ran the house. I don't think my father, who was ten years older than mother, liked this arrangement. We had a disturbed childhood.'

It was a big family and the lack of resources kept flaring up. Guru's father was struggling to make ends meet. The clerical post at the Burmah Shell Company paid the bills, but his dreams of a creative life were shattered. It left him a bitter and frustrated man.

Lalitha recalls, 'There were always financial problems. My father's job was low income. He was a clerk and he never rose to become any senior director [never rose to a senior position]. He was not ambitious. Perhaps he did not believe in success. A very idealistic man. He believed in poetry which is not enough to survive.

'My parents would often have heated arguments. Mother was very ambitious but my father was quite happy with his Keats, Shakespeare and Shaw. A laidback intellectual, he didn't talk much,'[9] recalled Lalitha. Guru Dutt and his siblings were scared of their father's temper and could never get close to him emotionally. As a kid, Guru was stubborn and short tempered like his father.

'Mother was the driving force. My father was very detached from the kids. He was never ever interested. Never even asked Ammaa how she was running the house. Once our school called him for a meeting but when he went there he had no clue in which class his kids were,' laughs Lalitha.

So it was Vasanthi who became the guiding light for her kids, especially Guru Dutt. He was the apple of her eye.

'Guru Dutt was also always quiet, aloof, always lost in his own world, dreaming his own dreams. He was never a talkative child. He shared a lot with my mother when he was a kid. But he remained quiet most of the time later.'

Hidden in the nooks and crannies of their modest existence, the little Guru Dutt was like a seeker with many questions. He had a habit of asking question after question until he got answers which satisfied his curiosities. He was a bright student at school and was fascinated by different languages, like Vasanthi. He spoke Hindi, Konkani and Bengali very well but was always more comfortable in English. At home, the family used to speak in Konkani and English. 'Guru's hobby was to collect books. He was a bookworm. I collected a few coins and encouraged him to buy second hand books. He started reading books from the age of 4 years. Beside our house there was a huge open space where Bengali jatras were performed. These jatras are like dramas without stage. Guru would never miss the jatra. By this time he could speak and understand Bengali.'

Jatra is a form of itinerant (gypsy) theatre that drew upon stories from epics and folk-tales, often with a view to impart a reformist, social or religious message. It was immensely popular in Bengal in the eighteenth and nineteenth centuries. Young Guru Dutt was fascinated with the performers telling stories from the Ramayana and the Mahabharata all night long. His mother recalled, 'This was his first exposure to storytelling. Imitating the Jatra performers, Guru would tie a cloth around him like a dhoti and would try to tell stories to his siblings.'[10]

Sitting at the door of his Bhowanipur house, young Guru Dutt often keenly watched the Baul singers of Calcutta, who played their ektaras and sang devotional songs on the streets. In the evening, his Nani would be lighting the diyas[11] for the evening aarti.[12] Guru Dutt, now a teenager, would make shadow figures of a swan or a deer in the flickering light of the diyas. Lalitha remembers, '...he was obsessed with shadow plays and would make numerous figures on the walls.'

More than anything else, Guru Dutt had a profound interest in dance. Uday Shankar's dance dramas used to be very popular in Calcutta. Guru Dutt happened to watch one of Shankar's shows at a very young age. 'After the day he watched his first Uday Shankar dance drama a great change came over him. Uday Shankar's virtuosity mesmerised him, he was inspired,' said Lalitha.[13] He was so enthralled that he told his mother, 'One day I want to be a dancer like him.'

But most importantly, it was in Calcutta that Guru met the person who would introduce him to the world of cinema and recognise his phenomenal talent. He would give him a dream—of recognising his inner artist and capabilities.

His name was B.B. Benegal.

Section Two

DESTRUCTION OF A DREAM

1956–57: BOMBAY

'The films he was making also affected him.'

3

THE THIRST

BOMBAY, 1956

'*Pyaasa*'s theme was inspired by my father.'

—Lalitha Lajmi

India was recently free from a long British rule of two centuries. There were dreams of a new nation, a better India. The 1950s, often termed as the 'Golden Era' of Indian cinema, witnessed films like Raj Kapoor's *Awaara* (1951) and *Shree 420* (1955), Satyajit Ray's *Pather Panchali* (1955), Chetan Anand's *Taxi Driver* (1954), Bimal Roy's *Do Bigha Zameen* (1953) and *Devdas* (1955), V. Shantaram's *Do Aaankehn Barah Hath*—all much talked about for the social concerns they brought to fore. Three actors were ruling the Hindi film industry—the triumverate of Dilip–Dev–Raj. Each one with a distinct style of their own and each one from a Punjabi-speaking background.

By 1956 Guru Dutt had secured his place as a promising filmmaker with four big successes as a director—*Baazi*, *Aar*

Paar, *Mr & Mrs 55* and *C.I.D.* The commercial success brought within reach all the dreams that the thirty-one-year-old Guru Dutt had harboured since his days in Calcutta.

The time had come to realise these dreams.

Guru Dutt had by then had achieved the quintessential tinsel town success—a bungalow in the posh Pali Hill area of Bombay, marriage and children with the legendary singer Geeta Roy and his own film banner as a producer-director-actor—Guru Dutt Films Pvt Ltd.

This finally catapulted him to pick the story he had been waiting to tell on the big screen for more than a decade—the classic, *Pyaasa*.[14]

Pyaasa was a personal story inspired by his early days in Bombay as well as the struggles faced by his father. His father's lifelong ambition was to engage in creative writing but he could only become a clerk. This exasperation he felt manifested itself in a childhood marred with his bitterness, reclusion and constant fights in the house for Guru Dutt and his siblings. He never could grow out of the need to be the breadwinner of the family and engage in creative pursuits.

Lalitha Lajmi said, 'Yes, *Pyaasa*'s theme was inspired by my father. Father was very creative and well-read...Guru Dutt inherited my father's temperament.'

Guru Dutt had written the story sometime in 1947. This was the time when India had just achieved independence but was suffering the bloody aftermath of the Partition. A twenty-two-year-old Guru Dutt had come to Bombay and lived with his family in a small rented flat and was struggling to make ends meet. This was also the time when he had realised how difficult it was for a creative man to survive or to make a place in the cut-throat culture of the film industry. He went door to door of many film producers but couldn't get work for almost a year. In that frame of mind, he wrote the story about the frustrations and anguish of an artist and called it 'Kashmakash'. The same story became *Pyaasa* ten years later with some crucial changes in the plot.

'You will realise that though he made it ten years later [after writing the story] he always wanted to make *Pyaasa* but there was less commercial angle so he was a little hesitant and the distributors kept on dissuading him,' Guru Dutt's son Arun Dutt had said in an interview.

The subject of *Pyaasa*, despite being extremely close to his heart, went through a whole process of to-do-or-not-to-do. He had already tasted success in the Bombay film industry riding on the popularity of mainstream romantic comedies and thrillers inspired from Hollywood. But in his heart, he longed to tell a tale that would establish him as an artistic and serious film-maker. But he was not confident. So before taking up *Pyaasa,* Guru Dutt had toyed with half-hearted ideas of other projects. Here's what was announced in the *Screen India* magazine before he announced *Pyaasa*:

Guru Dutt's next venture will be based on a famous Bengali poem.

This announcement was followed by another one indicating that the idea has been scrapped:

> Guru Dutt has put off the idea of making a popular Tagore poem into a film as reported earlier.

He was now working on a new idea. The announcement in *Screen India* said:

> Guru Dutt's next, the life story of a diver will be launched this month. Mostly it will be shot on location at Calcutta and in the Ganges River, the backdrop of the story written by Suhrid Kar, Chief Assistant of composer S.D. Burman. Guru Dutt will play the role of a diver. Hemant Kumar will compose the music.

And then an unexpected collaboration with the legendary director of *Mother India*, Mehboob Khan, was reported too:

> Guru Dutt is likely to direct a film for Mehboob Khan.

This perpetual indecisiveness remained Guru Dutt's Achilles' heel throughout his career and to an extent in his personal life too. Spending time on these ideas also meant wasting a lot of resources and money without any visible achievement. But writer and close associate, Abrar Alvi, who was part of Guru's A-team, clearly said money was just a means for Guru Dutt and never the end. He said, 'Nobody could ever have cared less for money. I have seen him squandering lakhs—not for personal indulgence but for his art. So many artists were signed and paid but never utilised, so many stories were bought which never went on the floors, so many films which went on the floors were never finished.'

Guru Dutt was busy working on the script of *Pyaasa* with Abrar Alvi. They were spending more time at Guru's house and sometimes at the farmhouse writing the screenplay. Abrar said, 'Those days, I would go home with Guru Dutt every evening and we would sit around with a drink each, discussing work. We started with *C.I.D.*, then the story and picturisation of *Pyaasa* took over our lives. And it was in those long fruitful evenings that I learnt a lot about Guru Dutt's technique and cinematic expression. He was a man obsessed with cinema.'

That obsession—added with his new-found success—was a heady cocktail. Guru Dutt now had money and clout. He now wanted to be recognised as a filmmaker with a difference. With two hit films as a lead actor, he could have opted to work as a hero in films outside his banner. It would have been an easier, more comfortable and starry career choice. But he had a deep desire to create films—artistic films. Having his own film production banner boosted his status as a successful producer. It also suited his temperament of shooting over long periods of time.

But running a company meant incurring huge costs and a regular flow of money was required for maintenance and salaries. A creative soul, Guru Dutt always found himself more at home with story ideas, song situations and creating magical moments on celluloid; however, as the studio boss he was also required to give his time to the administrative and financial health of his company. His trusted chief production controller, Guruswamy, handled the day-to-day functioning of the studio.

He also felt responsible for his staff. So many families depended on him for their livelihood. So it was important that his company should produce successful films regularly. There were bonuses when a film did well. His kindness was duly acknowledged by people who worked with him. 'There was a certain nobility about him. Once an artiste who had been helped on many occasions, monetarily or otherwise began to give constant trouble. Once I pulled him up and reminded him of the help we had given him on many occasions. Later, Guru Dutt called me to his office and told me, "Never mention about helping someone. It hurts human pride,"' recalled Guruswamy.[15]

But while it wasn't possible for Guru Dutt to shoot every day, it was important that his staff had regular work even when he was busy planning his next film. For that, the company had to churn out more films on a regular basis, even if it meant hiring directors. Also, it was of prime importance to produce commercially viable films first and then invest in artistic 'dream projects' like *Pyaasa*. So Guru Dutt decided to follow a simple rule: in his production company each commercially successful film would be followed by a 'risky and artistic' film. Commercial success was always very important to Guru Dutt.

Guru Dutt had already begun shooting a few sequences of *Pyaasa* when his previous film, *C.I.D.*, was being made. He had filmed three reels but wasn't satisfied with what he had shot. So he scrapped the entire footage and decided to shoot it again.

Pyaasa, which literally means 'the thirsty', was finally

in the making. With this dream project, Guru Dutt perhaps also set off on a path of unquenchable creative perfection—eventually derailing every other dream he held close.

4

DILIP KUMAR AND *PYAASA*

'Guru Dutt was hesitant to face the camera as an actor.'

—V.K. Murthy

For his most ambitious film yet, *Pyaasa*, Guru Dutt wanted the best actor around. He wanted the 'tragedy king', the top star of the 1950s—Dilip Kumar. Dilip was known to take his craft extremely seriously and was a perfectionist to the core. He normally worked in one film at a time to give it his 100 per cent. This was exactly the kind of dedication Guru Dutt wanted from his *Pyaasa* hero.

Guru went to meet Dilip Kumar and narrated the script of *Pyaasa* to him. Dilip Kumar agreed to do the film in principle. He quoted his price of one-and-a-half-lakh rupees. Guru Dutt requested him to consider reducing the price as he had already scrapped the shoot he had done for the film, wasting a considerable amount. In reply, he was asked not to worry about the money. Now that Dilip Kumar was to take on the lead role, his loyal film distributors would take care of the finances. This perhaps was the point where

Guru Dutt disagreed with him. Guru Dutt clearly told Dilip Kumar that he had a fixed team of distributors too and he had committed *Pyaasa* to them. In Sathya Saran's book *Ten Years with Guru Dutt*, Abrar Alvi says that Guru Dutt told Dilip Kumar, 'I haven't come to you to sell my film. I can sell it on my own. I have come to you as a director, because I believe that if I cast you in my film, I will make a better film. You will add stature to it.'[16]

Whether Dilip Kumar, the biggest star-actor of those times, took offense is not known. Dilip Kumar never talked about this meeting ever. But at that time he promised Guru Dutt that he would come for the shooting from the next day.

The following day, all preparations were done for the muhurat[17] shot. The entire unit of *Pyaasa* was waiting to welcome their star, Dilip Kumar. Hours passed but Kumar didn't arrive.

Guru Dutt's production controller and confidante Guruswamy said, 'I myself had gone to fetch Dilip Saab. But he was not to be found at home.'

Guru's brother, Devi Dutt recalls, 'He [Dilip Kumar] was to attend the mahurat at A.P. Kardar Studio. Also, [producer–director] B.R. Chopra's office was in the same compound. Dilip Saab went there to meet him. There was a quiet rivalry between B.R. Chopra Saab and Guru Dutt. Dilip Saab sat there discussing the script of Chopra Saab's *Naya Daur* as the mahurat time (of *Pyaasa*) slipped by. Guru Dutt sent for him. Dilip Saab said he'd be there in ten minutes.' But even then Dilip Kumar did not turn up.

Around lunch time, Guru Dutt sent for two bees.

By 3 pm he had decided to play the protagonist himself and took the first shot—a close-up shot of a bee thirsty for nectar but a man passing by crushes the innocent life under his foot.[18]

Guru Dutt had always underestimated himself as an actor. In all his films where he had played the lead role, he was always the reluctant second or third choice. Cinematographer and another of Guru Dutt's A-team members, V.K. Murthy remembered, 'He was hesitant to face the camera as actor… He could not critique his acting adequately, and so this job was up to Abrar or I.'[19]

There were always talks of signing other actors for the role. In *Pyaasa* too, after scrapping the initial shoot with himself in the lead role, he had started thinking that he didn't possess the histrionics required for the very complex role of the tragic poet. He felt that a craftier actor was needed.

Later, Dilip Kumar said in an interview that he didn't sign *Pyaasa* as his role was similar to the one he had played in his memorable film *Devdas*. He never mentioned anything else on record. It's true that had Dilip Kumar turned up on that fateful day, *Pyaasa* would have been a very different film. But the way in which Guru Dutt played the role of Vijay, it is difficult to imagine anyone except him in that role now. He gave it his everything. Guru Dutt became Vijay, the heartbroken poet.

The audacious move by Guru Dutt to take on the role that Dilip Kumar refused paid off and it became 'one of Bollywood's all-time greatest performances'. Bunny Reuben, the biographer of the thespian Dilip Kumar writes, 'What, in fact, Guru Dutt had actually done, was to…inform the entire cinema-going world that he had given a "Dilip Kumar role" to a totally new actor and he'd made a super-hit out of his film.' There cannot be a more telling statement on the feat that had been achieved.

With himself in the lead male role, the quest for the female lead started.

5

AN ACCIDENT AND WAHEEDA REHMAN

'That meeting appeared to be just a coincidence; but destiny must have known that my days were changed…'

—Waheeda Rehman

The casting of the female leads for *Pyaasa* went through many changes. Initially Madhubala was considered to play the role that finally went to Mala Sinha. Meenu Mumtaz was signed as the streetwalker's friend while the song 'Jaane kya tune kahi' was to be picturised on Kumkum. However, in the final cut, both Meenu Mumtaz and Kumkum were out.

A relatively new actress, Waheeda Rehman, was finalised to play the lead role of the prostitute, Gulabo, opposite the protagonist, poet Vijay (Guru Dutt). Initially Guru Dutt's team wasn't happy with her casting. It was a complex role that required a mature and seasoned actress and Waheeda was just one film old. But Guru Dutt had absolutely no doubt. Abrar Alvi said[20] that in the beginning at least the romantic in Guru Dutt saw in Waheeda the perfect foil to his creative and intellectual leanings.

Guru Dutt's cinema wasn't the same after he met Waheeda. But how he met Waheeda was sheer destiny.

In the small town of Chengalpattu, forty-five miles from Madras city (Tamil Nadu), Waheeda Rehman was born on 3 February 1938/39. Her father, Mohd Abdur Rehman was a district commissioner and mother, Mumtaz Begum, a homemaker. Waheeda was the youngest of four sisters. At the age of nine, Waheeda, along with her sisters, went to learn Bharatnatyam at Rajmundry. But then tragedy struck.

Waheeda's father passed away when she was only thirteen years old. With no regular earning now, Waheeda and her elder sister Sayeeda began performing on stage but the earning wasn't enough to sustain their family. Then a close family friend, film producer Ramakrishna Prasad, offered Waheeda a song-and-dance number in his Telugu film *Rojulu Marayi* (which means 'times have changed'). The song was a chartbuster and through her dance Waheeda became an overnight star. It was through this song that Waheeda Rehman met Guru Dutt and then went on to play a crucial part in his life.

And it happened in Hyderabad.

Guru Dutt's distributor from the south of India told him about a Telugu film, *Misiamma*, that was a runaway hit there. He suggested that it could be a good idea to remake the film in Hindi. He asked Guru Dutt to come to Hyderabad and watch the film that was running to packed theatres. Guru Dutt agreed.

It was decided that it would be a road trip to Hyderabad in Guru Dutt's car. Abrar Alvi and Guruswamy would give him company. They left the same evening, drove right through the night and reached Hyderabad the next morning. But then there was an accident. The driver was tired and smashed the car into a buffalo. No one was hurt except Guru Dutt's Plymouth car. It had severely broken down and the mechanic told them it would take three days to repair it. The one-day-film-watching-trip was now accidentally extended to three days. What's worse, Guru Dutt finally watched *Misiamma* and did not like it. He was now irritated at such a total waste of a trip with nothing coming out of it. But he had two more days in hand. To kill time he went to meet one of his film distributors and then, fate intervened.

Guru Dutt and Abrar Alvi were sitting in the office of the distributor when they noticed a commotion outside. Guru Dutt was keenly watching some youngsters as they surrounded a car that had stopped over there. The door opened and a girl came out of the car. Guru Dutt looked at the distributor quizzically. 'She is Waheeda Rehman,' he told Guru Dutt, adding that the girl had performed only a dance number in the film *Rojulu Marayi* but that dance number had become a sensation. The film was a smashing success making the dancer, Waheeda, popular among the youngsters.

It was fate playing its hand. Waheeda was based out of Madras but had come to Hyderabad for the success event of *Rojulu Marayi* at the same time that Guru was on an unplanned visit to Hyderabad.

Waheeda Rehman remembered, '*Rojulu Marayi* had completed its 100th day run in Hyderabad. Mr Guru Dutt happened to be in Hyderabad at that time and had seen a big crowd outside the theatre.'

Guru Dutt was surprised, 'Waheeda Rehman? That's a Muslim name. Does she speak Urdu?' He asked the distributor to arrange a meeting. 'I had not seen his movies or even heard his name till then; I did not know who he was.' The next day, Waheeda came with her mother for the meeting. Her first meeting with Guru Dutt.

Waheeda Rehman seemed nothing like the sensation as described by the distributor. She was plainly dressed and spoke very little. Guru Dutt too didn't speak much. He asked about her background, if she could speak Urdu and if she had learnt dancing. Waheeda replied in monosyllables. In some time the meeting ended. Recalling their first meeting Waheeda said, 'He hardly spoke a sentence or two when I met him for the first time in 1955. That meeting appeared to be just a coincidence; but destiny must have known that my days were changed…"days are changed" translated in Telegu, the language of my first movie, would be *Rojulu Marayi*.'

The distributor also suggested that Guru Dutt must watch her dance number from *Rojulu Marayi* before leaving for Bombay. The reel was arranged. Meanwhile Guru Dutt and friends spent the afternoon quaffing beer and having lunch. Abrar Alvi narrates in writer Sathya Saran's book *Ten Years with Guru Dutt*, 'By the time we got to the projection room we had downed six bottles, and, more likely than not, were in happy haze. The reel was shown, the dance number was fast paced and well-executed, but there was not a single shot of the dancer in close-up. "How is she?" Guru Dutt asked, "Very photogenic," I replied. "I also think so," Guru Dutt opined.'

That was it. They didn't discuss Waheeda after that. The car was repaired and they came back to Bombay. Guru Dutt was now more worried that they wasted so much time due to the accident just for the film *Misiamma* for which he had actually gone to Hyderabad. He wasn't going to remake it. It also meant that Guru Dutt had nothing in hand to make before *Pyaasa*.

Waheeda later said, 'I did not give any importance to that meeting and forgot all about it. But he did not.'

Few months later, Guru Dutt gave Waheeda Rehman a break by casting her in a side role in his film *C.I.D.*, but her song and dance act 'Kahin pe nigahein, kahin pe nishana' became a runaway hit and outshone even the lead actress, Shakila. Film magazines announced that impressed by Waheeda Rehman, Guru Dutt had given her a crucial role in his ambitious project *Pyaasa*.

The new mentor-protégé relationship was already being talked about in the corridors of the film industry.

6

INDECISIONS AND GURU

'The kind of serious films he was making had also affected him. His personality had changed.'

—Lalitha Lajmi

Pyaasa, in a truly mainstream format, raises critical questions. The socio-romantic melodrama had all the elements that were considered an intrinsic part of Hindi cinema of those times. But with Guru Dutt's understated craft, important issues were blended within the film with sophistication and subtlety. The film repeatedly questioned the system that was so cold-blooded and discouraging for artists. What is more relevant—money or art? The questions that had also troubled Guru Dutt's father. *Pyaasa* raised these questions on a materialistic society through a story which was hard-hitting, haunting, artistic yet entertaining and well within the mainstream format. This is what made *Pyaasa* everlastingly relevant.

Professor Ira Bhaskar says, 'Guru Dutt was an auteur, a mainstream cinema auteur. There's no doubt about it. Also,

1950 is a very interesting phase in Indian cinema in a sense that Guru Dutt's work is a critique of the nationalism and national agenda. Like in *Pyaasa*. It is surprising *Pyaasa* was a successful film, considering it was an extremely critical film about Indian capitalism. The two scathing songs—"Jinhe naaz hai hind par wo kahaan hain" and "Ye duniya agar mil bhi jaaye to kya hai". The songs that are still completely relevant after six decades. There is also a running metaphor in the film: prostitution, which is not really about a prostitute but in a way about how capitalism prostitutes everything. That sets him apart from say Mehboob Khan, another great filmmaker of that time. But there is also a similarity with someone like K.A. Abbas. Abbas was writing for filmmaker-actor Raj Kapoor. There were similarities in social concerns and issues in films like *Shri 420* and *Awara*.'

As an actor, Guru Dutt gave his soul to the role of the tormented poet Vijay. He believed that the eyes were the most expressive part of a person and they spoke more than anything else. When you recall any famous Guru Dutt photograph, or any of his scenes from a film, you will instantly remember his intense eyes. But a fact often overlooked is that Guru Dutt used to wear thick eyeglasses due to poor eyesight. While in front of the camera, however, he used to remove the glasses to look natural. It, in fact, worried him that he did not have the capabilities of projecting intense expressions through his eyes. He may have not been able to see the camera clearly without glasses but he worked really hard to express through his eyes. And the magic was there for all to see.

More than sixty years have passed but you utter the word *Pyaasa* and what comes to mind are the songs, and the way Guru Dutt captured and immortalised them.[21] Lyrics and poetry by Sahir was put to tunes remarkably by S.D. Burman. The song sequences were replete with symbolisms that have been repeatedly decoded over the years. The shot-taking practices prevalent in Indian cinema at that time were mid-shots and long shots. Guru Dutt was perhaps the first to use an establishing shot followed by close-ups in his films. He was obsessed with close-ups and extensively used long focal-length lenses (75 mm and 100 mm). Even after so many decades, those close-up shots stand out. Devi Dutt remembers, 'The close-up shots with a 100 mm lens in his films, which became known as the "Guru Dutt shot", the masterful play with light and even his melancholia soaked frames, still enthrall cineastes.'[22]

Most songs in the film begin in the true Guru Dutt tradition—without introductory music. The songs were an extension of the conversations in the script. V.K. Murthy recounted, 'His filming of songs and scenes was unique. Others just used to keep the camera fixed, have the actors perform the song, walking in or out of frame and have a few cut to close-up shots, that's all. But Guru Dutt was not like that at all. He emphasised movements and that too in close-up shots.' He undoubtedly had a very good sense of movement owing to his dance training at Uday Shankar's Dance Centre.

Having closely observed the Baul singers in the streets of Calcutta as a child, he recreated the imagery in the song 'Aaj saajan mohe ang laga lo'—a devotional love song where the desire of the lover is projected as spiritual and divine.

Guru Dutt's obsession with Bengal can be clearly seen in *Pyaasa*. He wanted to shoot in Calcutta so some scenes were rewritten to include locations from the city in the story. This led to an amusing incident. Actor Mehmood was cast in *Pyaasa*, as Guru Dutt's elder brother. It was the scene of their mother's last rites and the location was the Calcutta Ghats. Abrar Alvi was responsible for the dialogues and accent of the actors but on this particular day he was absent from the shoot. Mehmood asked the location of the shot and when told that it was to be shot at the Calcutta Ghats, he decided to say his dialogues in a Bengali accent, whereas the rest of the family spoke in a North Indian/ Benares accent. The scene is still there in the film.

People close to Guru Dutt have gone on record to say that he did not believe in shooting a film with a bound script or strict planning of shooting schedules. He was rather fond of 'creating' the film as it took shape on the sets, making a lot of changes in the script and dialogues. Abrar Alvi had said that Guru Dutt shot the film in random order and the raw stock Guru Dutt used for any one film could have finished three films.

Veteran lyricist and film producer Amit Khanna who worked closely with Dev Anand says, 'Guru Dutt was the kind of filmmaker who reshot a lot of his stuff. So he was a very expensive filmmaker. There were others like Raj Kapoor, Ramesh Sippy, Manoj Kumar who shot and scrapped but Guru Dutt was at some other level. He would scrap films he had shot for months. Very indecisive.'

By the time he made *Pyaasa*, the indecisiveness had magnified manifold. He would shoot and shoot and was unsure about what he really wanted in a particular scene. Even with himself, for the famous climax sequence in *Pyaasa*, he shot one-hundred and four takes! He kept forgetting the dialogues as it was a very lengthy shot, but he wanted it just right...he would shout and get bad-tempered when things did not go right. Before *Pyaasa*, he would scrap only one or two shots of a film, rather than entire sequences. But beginning from *Pyaasa*, the scrapping and reshooting had reached worrying new levels. People close to him noticed this change. However, it was attributed to the reason that with his dream project *Pyaasa*, Guru Dutt did not want to leave any stone unturned.

He wanted it to be perfect.

Sleep evaded him. The misuse of and dependence on alcohol had begun. At his worst, he started experimenting with sleeping pills, mixing them in his whiskey.

Remembering those days, Lalitha Lajmi told this author, 'The kind of serious films he was making had also affected him. His personality had changed. He had become more reclusive…sometimes he used to call me saying he wants to talk about something. But whenever I went to meet him, he never really confided. He was disturbed.'

Guru Dutt gave his all to make *Pyaasa*—his sleep, his dreams, and the memories of his childhood.

Section Three

BUILDING OF A DREAM

1931–47: CALCUTTA TO MUMBAI

'Guru Dutt was a romantic really.'

7

AU REVOIR, CALCUTTA

> 'More than anyone else it was uncle Benegal who influenced Guru Dutt immensely. He was Guru Dutt's first mentor.'
>
> —Lalitha Lajmi

It is said a life is not important except in the impact it has on other lives. B.B. Benegal had that seminal impact on Guru Dutt's childhood.

It was an aged building on 183, Dharamtalla Street, near Jyoti cinema, one of the oldest cinema halls in Calcutta. That is where B.B. Benegal lived.

'I still have dreams of Uncle Benegal's house on Dharamtalla Street. Guru, Atma, cousin Jaya, the dog Bobby, and I spent memorable moments there. Uncle Benegal was a very kind man,' says Lalitha.

B.B. Benegal was Guru Dutt's mother Vasanthi's favourite cousin. While Guru's father slogged at his work, it was uncle Benegal who took great care of the the family and kids. 'My uncle was very close to us and you know he was a film publicist and he used to live next to Jyoti cinema. And he used to do publicity for English, Hindi and Bengali films. So publicity means artwork. He was a commercial artist as well as a painter. In those days taking painting or poetry as a profession was not possible,' remembered Lalitha.

Benegal had a large studio, and downstairs were his living quarters. The kids used to spend many weekends in his house. 'Because of the publicity he was doing for films, he used to get free passes to see those films. My grandmother used to take us by tram every Friday. Saturday and Sunday we used to stay there. Our favourites were the Walt Disney movies. There was a time when Guru Dutt as a child used to see three movies in a day—Hindi, Bangla and English films,' said Lalitha remembering those early days.

B.B. Benegal was a commercial artist and photographer and he used to design and paint film hoardings in Calcutta.

'More than anyone else it was uncle Benegal who influenced Guru Dutt immensely. He was Guru Dutt's first mentor,' shared sister Lalitha. Benegal realised that Guru Dutt loved music and had a natural affinity towards dancing. Guru Dutt loved S.D. Burman's Bengali music and used to play his songs repeatedly on Benegal's gramophone. When Benegal was not around, Guru used to take his camera from Banegal's wife to photograph animals in the Calcutta zoo. 'He fidgeted with the camera and proudly told us all that one day he, too, would make a film.' Benegal never told him that he couldn't. Unlike Guru Dutt's father, in Benegal's world, dreams were not just allowed, they were encouraged.

'Benegal Uncle gave my brother a Bosch camera when he was young and a box of colours to me when I was five. Very symbolic because he became a filmmaker and I, an artist. I was very close to Guru Dutt because I think it was art that binded us. Both of us had an artistic bent of mind. So we understood each other,' said Lalitha.

To make ends meet Vasanthi gave private tuitions. B.B. Benegal said to her, 'Leave Guru Dutt to me, I will look after him.' He removed Guru from the South Indian school he was studying in as he was not doing well there and put him in David Hare's English-medium school. There, Guru was quite happy and became a good student.

Guru Dutt passed his matriculation in 1941 and his mother Vasanthi, who also had decided to continue her education passed her high school in 1940, a year before her son. Guru Dutt was always in awe of his mother. She also obtained a diploma in Education and later took up a teaching job. While her husband was a master of one language, she, through her passion for learning became well versed in eight languages. Vasanthi wrote for magazines, and years later even translated a Bengali novel *Mithun* to Kannada.

But the family was going through a major financial crunch. Being the eldest son, Guru Dutt had to discontinue his studies after high school to supplement his father's income. He was sixteen.

Guru Dutt joined as a telephone operator on a monthly salary of forty rupees. But the job made him really restless and he left it after a month and a half. Lalitha laughed, 'He hated the job so much that by the end of the month he did not even go to collect his month's pay.'

Guru Dutt then joined Hindustan Lever's Calcutta office at a monthly salary of rupees thirty. 'He was extremely generous. When he got his first salary he bought gifts for everyone in the family. A dress for me, saris for Amma [mother] and grandmother and a copy of the *Bhagwad Gita* for his teacher. But despite all this we knew he felt trapped in a daily job.'

It was B.B. Benegal again who came to his rescue. This time it was a painting by him that inspired Guru Dutt.

The painting had a man holding a snake coiled around his body. Benegal had named it 'The Struggle for Existence'. Benegal recalled, 'When Guru Dutt saw the painting, he said, "Uncle, I feel like dancing to this!"'[23] Guru jumped with joy when he suggested they shoot the same dance performance on their 8 mm colour camera.

On a November morning, with the sun rising in the background, Benegal took Guru Dutt to the famous Eden Gardens in Calcutta to capture 'The Snake Charmer' dance on camera. An excited Guru Dutt put Benegal's red shawl on his head and tied a yellow cloth around his waist. He also put on some make-up. Then he began dancing. There was no music, yet he was dancing gracefully to a silent tune. Captured on an old 8 mm camera, this was young Guru Dutt's dance to freedom. B.B. Benegal reminisces in

Nasreen Munni Kabir's book *Guru Dutt: A Life in Cinema*, 'He looked just like a snake charmer. There was no music playing as he was dancing; he was just *thinking* the music.'[24]

The dance inspired by Benegal's painting really acted as a catalyst. The performance captured on camera gave him the confidence to finally take the plunge. His heart had decided that he would be a dancer. With the help of a few friends, Guru Dutt managed to get an appointment with Uday Shankar and gave a secret audition. More than the performance it was the infectious passion for dance and determination on Guru's face that struck Shankar. As soon as the dance performance was over, Uday Shankar announced, 'Come to Almora.'

But the family had no money to pay the fee. It was B.B. Benegal again who came to the rescue. With the help of his film distributor friend, S.R. Hemmad, he managed to get a scholarship of Rs 75 for Guru Dutt to go and study at Uday Shankar's dance centre. The path was now clear. Guru had tears in his eyes.

'Take the blankets because it is very cold in Almora. If you have any difficulties, just write to me,' said B.B. Benegal, Guru Dutt's first mentor, Santa Claus and fairy rolled into one.

It was time to say goodbye to Calcutta, his soul-city.

8

DANCE WHEN YOU'RE BROKEN

ALMORA, 1942

'At Uday Shankar's dance centre, I saw how complex life is, and how simple too.'

—Guru Dutt

It was at the Uday Shankar India Culture Centre in Almora (earstwhile U.P.) where Guru Dutt imbibed his sense of rhythm, music and power of images. Popularly known as the father of modern dance, Uday Shankar was born in an affluent Bengali family. Though he never had any formal training in dance, he worked for over a decade with the famous Russian ballerina Anna Pavlova.

In 1938, Uday Shankar decided to make India his base, and established the 'Uday Shankar India Cultural Centre', at Simtola, 3 km from Almora.[25] His aim was to popularise and propagate classical Indian dance forms. He invited various dancers and musicians to teach Kathakali, Bharatnatyam, Kathak and other dance forms. Soon the centre began to attract students from across the country.

Guru Dutt joined at the end of 1941 at the age of sixteen. He soon became one of Uday Shankar's favourite students. He was the youngest and the best-looking man at the centre with jet black hair, a calm face and an innocence that was hard to miss. He knew how to use the camera so Uday Shankar gave him his camera to capture the images at the centre. Guru Dutt felt at home. Later he shared[26], 'I used to get impressed by simple things. I saw how complex life is, and how simple too.'

Vasanthi recalled, 'Sometimes I felt nervous as I did not know what Guru Dutt's future would be…that was the first time when we were separated from each other. Guru felt our separation very much, although he was busy with his own work and was happy.'

At the centre, the focus was not only on producing dancers but all-round artists. The centre was like a huge commune where the students had to maintain strict discipline. They had yoga classes, literature and psychology training. They had to create their own dance themes, stitch their own costumes and create plays and performances. In a play based on the Ramayana, Guru Dutt had essayed the role of Lakshman. These shows were performed as shadow plays too. It was here that Guru Dutt learnt to adjust the lights to make a figure appear small or large.

While Guru Dutt was well settled in Almora, his family in Calcutta was again being uprooted.

In 1942, during the Second World War, there were rumours of Calcutta being bombed by the Japanese. Vasanthi left the city with her children to stay with her brother-in-law in Karnataka. Soon Burmah Shell Company also decided to move their offices to Bombay. Shivshankar Padukone was also transferred. In August 1942, Vasanthi and the kids also came to Bombay. They shifted to a flat in Matunga in Bombay, the city which remained home to Guru Dutt for the rest of his life.

In December 1942, Uday Shankar brought his troupe to perform in Bombay. Guru Dutt's performance was at the Excelsior theatre and he sent passes to his family. It was the first time that Guru's parents and siblings watched him perform on stage with dancers. 'He must be seventeen, had an extremely fair complexion and jet black, long hair. He performed his swan dance. Our family was so happy for him,' remembers Lalitha.

But the beautiful Uday Shankar chapter in Guru Dutt's life was also coming to an end.

Due to the war, the foreign funding to Uday Shankar's India Culture Centre became difficult to sustain and it finally closed down in 1944. This was a huge jolt for all the students, including Guru Dutt. His mother wrote in her memoir, 'One evening Guru returned with three of his colleagues with bag and baggage...we were all keenly disappointed at the turn of events. The poor students did not know what they would do in future. They were all depressed.' Lalitha Lajmi added, 'Guru was one of his favourite students. Uday Shankar told my mother to make sure Guru should continue dancing. But we knew dance wasn't really a profession in those days. There was no future in dancing.'

At that time, Guru Dutt didn't know that sometimes things fall apart so better things can fall in place. The stint at Almora had taught him an important lesson: many times in life one has to lose things and people close to one's heart and have to learn to begin afresh. This cycle keeps repeating.

9

DEV ANAND, A FRIEND FOR LIFE

POONA, 1944–46

> 'We promised each other that the day I became a producer, I'd take him on as a director, and the day he directed a film, he'd cast me as a hero.'
>
> —Dev Anand

It was time to seek a new direction in life. After spending a few months in sheer desperation, twenty-year-old Guru Dutt turned to his mentor B.B. Benegal once again. Benegal took Guru Dutt to Poona and introduced him to Baburao Pai who was a partner in the famous Prabhat Film Company, popularly known as Prabhat Studios in Poona. The studio had a reputation of being an institution that produced successful films in the past and it was in the process of hiring new talent and revamping itself.

Guru Dutt was hired as a dance director at Prabhat Studio at a salary of Rs 50 a month, on a three year contract. He also worked as an assistant director and sometimes even as an actor in the films produced by Prabhat Studio. In the film *Lakharani* (1945), Guru Dutt appeared as one of the group dancers and also acted in a scene in which he was tied up and beaten. This was his first appearance as an actor. He was also an assistant to director Vishram Bedekar. 'It is possible,' said Atma Ram, 'that it was at this stage, while working in *Lakharani*, that Guru Dutt decided to become a director. Till then his goal was to pursue dancing in its pure or applied form.'

It was here in Poona, during the making of the 1946 film *Hum Ek Hain*, when he met friends who would play a very crucial role in his life and his films.

Coming from Lahore of undivided India, with dreams of becoming an actor, Dev Anand was struggling to get a foothold in the Bombay film industry. The year was 1946 when he met Baburao Pai of Prabhat Studio and managed to impress him after gate-crashing into his office. Pai gave Dev Anand a train ticket to Poona and asked him to give an audition in Prabhat Studio. Dev Anand gave a stylish audition and was selected for the film *Hum Ek Hain* to be directed by P.L. Santoshi. He was offered a monthly salary of Rs 350—a big amount in those days.

The shooting was about to begin in a few days. Dev Anand was staying in the guesthouse of Prabhat Film Company when one day there was a knock at the door.

'Kaun hai?' (Who is there?) asked Dev.

'Main kapde laya hoon,' (I've brought the clothes) said the washerman's young son, Tukaram.

Dev Anand came to the door of his room to take his clothes but realised that his favourite shirt was missing. There was another shirt which didn't belong to him: 'This is not my shirt! That dhobi, I'll sack him!' Dev shouted blaming the young boy's father.

The washerman's son was scared. Dev Anand asked him if he has delivered his shirt to some other room. Tukaram had no idea. In search of the shirt, they knocked on the door of a few rooms and finally a bespectacled young man, holding a book in his hand, came out from a room. Dev Anand explained the situation to him and asked if the man had got his shirt by mistake. The man smiled and confirmed that he had a similar 'wrong shirt' story and fortunately the shirt too.

They smiled. Dev introduced himself and said he was the lead actor of *Hum Ek Hain*.

Shaking hands with Dev Anand the bespectacled man replied, 'I am the lead choreographer of *Hum Ek Hain*. My name is Guru Dutt.' Dev recalled later, 'We had a hearty laugh and embraced each other. We were to be friends for all times.'

Guru Dutt was also the assistant director and even played a small role in *Hum Ek Hain*. The film was a two-hero story about Hindu-Muslim unity. Dev Anand played the Hindu character while the Muslim character was played by another young, good-looking actor, Rahman. Dev Anand, Rahman and Guru Dutt became close friends during the making of the film. They would cycle around the roads of Poona, cook together, watch movies together, share each other's secrets and were inseparable.

The twenty-one-year-old Guru Dutt felt at home with these new friends. He was also on a road of self-discovery, realising that it is filmmaking that was going to be his calling in life. Together they talked about their dreams, their future in films. During one such conversation Guru Dutt and Dev Anand made a promise: 'We promised each other that the day I became a producer, I'd take him on as a director, and the day he directed a film, he'd cast me as a hero,' said Dev Anand.

Guru Dutt and Dev Anand had crossed paths for a reason. The promise was for keeps.

10

THE HEARTBREAKS

'In Pune, he was involved with a girl of dubious reputation. They almost got married but then finally he broke off with her. I feel he always had a compassion for "fallen" women.'

—Lalitha Lajmi

There was love in the air too.

The shooting of *Hum Ek Hain* was on in full swing when Guru Dutt fell in love. Being a dance director, Guru came into contact with a dancer called Vijaya. One thing led to another and soon they were in a serious relationship. His mother writes, 'During Ganesh Puja, Guru Dutt gave us a surprise visit. He came along with Vijaya just when the puja was going on. They both came and touched my feet. Guru Dutt introduced her to me as my future daughter-in-law.' The family treated her as a family member. They were happy and wanted Guru Dutt to marry soon. Guru and Vijaya left the same evening.

And then the problems began.

Then next morning Vasanthi received a wire from a lawyer in Poona. The senior lawyer, Mr Khajigiwala, had written that Guru Dutt had eloped with Vijaya and he would take legal action against him. But Guru Dutt remained undaunted.

Then a strange thing happened. The wife of the lawyer, Mrs Khajigiwala, visited Vasanthi many times to get her permission for Guru Dutt's and Vijaya's wedding as Guru was legally underage by a few months and consent of the parents was important. But soon the story began to unfold. Vasanthi wrote, 'Later it was rumoured that Vijaya was Khajigiwala's mistress. His wife was jealous and wanted to separate Vijaya from her husband. She played all sorts of tricks to persuade us to consent to the marriage.'

The wedding date was fixed and announced in a Marathi daily newspaper without the parents' permission. The senior lawyer was after him. It could have got Guru Dutt arrested. So, a friend of Guru Dutt's advised Vasanthi to take him to Bombay immediately, averting the crisis.

Recalling the incident Lalitha said, 'Yes, in Pune, he was involved with a girl of dubious reputation. They almost got married but then finally he broke off with her. I feel he always had a compassion for "fallen" women.'

But Guru Dutt had contemplated a future with Vijaya and now he was heartbroken. His mother writes, 'I thought that it was better if Guru got married to somebody to save him from further calamities. So I chose my Hyderabad cousin's daughter, Suvarna, for him to marry.' Guru met Suvarna and liked her. They started writing letters to each other. It went on for some time. Vasanthi was happy that his son had moved on from that previous heartbreak. But then suddenly Suvarna's family stopped replying to their letters. 'They broke connections with us, and arranged the girl's marriage with another boy,' recalled Vasanthi.

Vasanthi soon realised the reason for her cousin's bizarre behaviour. Guru Dutt, in an attempt at being honest, had written to his uncle (Suvarna's father) about the Vijaya story. His intention was to avoid misunderstandings after marriage. Vasanthi wrote, 'Perhaps they lost confidence in Guru Dutt. We had that black spot for film line, as its reputation was bad at that time.' Suvarna's father was convinced that people working in the film industry had loose morals and his daughter would not be happy with Guru Dutt.

This was deemed as an insult to the family. For the sensitive Guru Dutt, it was the second heartbreak in quick succession. It affected him emotionally. Sadness engulfed him and he went silent. 'He never showed his feelings to anybody. But I could make out. The disappointment was too much for both of us,' wrote Vasanthi.

In Pune, Guru immersed himself in work. Dev Anand called Guru Dutt 'brimming over with artistic creation and lava that has to explode', but added that he was '…all the time at war with his inner self, melancholy and withdrawn.'

In the midst of this emotional turmoil, time had also come to say goodbye to Poona.

11

BOMBAY CALLING!

1947

The shooting of *Hum Ek Hain* was over. Baburao Pai had left Prabhat Film Company and started his own Famous Studios in Bombay where Guru Dutt was now given the job of assisting the director Anadinath Banerjee. At that time Banerjee was directing a film called *Mohan.* Dev Anand had also left Prabhat and shifted back to Bombay. He was signed as the hero of *Mohan.* The two friends were reunited. But the happiness didn't last long.

The year was 1947. Along with independence from the British rule, the country also witnessed the Partition. And with that the film industry was also partitioned. There was random migration of cinema talent between the two newly formed nations. India lost some luminaries and gained others. Around the same time, film-makers and actors from the Calcutta film industry began migrating to Bombay. As a result, Bombay became the center of film production in the Republic of India after Partition. On the night of independence, even the movie stars were euphoric. Dev

Anand took his car out and drove all around Churchgate in it. *Jugnu*, starring Dilip Kumar and Noor Jehan, was the most popular film released in 1947. Cinema legends like Raj Kapoor and Madhubala made their debut with Neel Kamal. The same year Dev Anand starred in two successful films—*Mohan* and *Aage Badho*. A new order was being established in the Bombay film industry.

But Dev's friend, the twenty-two-year-old Guru Dutt, was struggling to survive.

Guru Dutt's contract with Baburao Pai got over in 1947. He badly needed a job. He met many producers, knocked on the doors of many studious to get one. He even went to Madras to try his luck at Gemini Studios. But nothing worked. Lalitha said, 'He was out of work and frustrated. He started writing. He wrote some short stories and mailed to the famous *The Illustrated Weekly of India.* The editor used to be an Englishman, S.R. Mandy. But none of his stories were published. They all came back with a rejection slip.'

It had been almost a year with rejection written all over his life. He had tried securing a job as a choreographer, writer, assistant director but felt there was no one who could understand the heart of an artist. In his young mind he thought everyone was interested in making money and no one cared for the art. This disturbed the sensitive Guru very much. He became so disillusioned that he planned on opening a bookshop with his brother Atmaram. He could have turned to his mentor B.B. Benegal for direction, but Calcutta was seeing frightening communal riots and it had taken a toll on Benegal. It was during this turbulent phase that Guru Dutt began writing a story based on the conflict going on in his mind and soul. He aptly called it 'Kashmakash' (Conflict).

The story was written at a producer's office while waiting for work. His son Arun Dutt said, 'There was a period in 1947 where he was out of work for nearly eight to ten months. So at that time he used to go to some producer's office quite often, because the original story of *Pyaasa*, I have a copy, is handwritten on the letterhead of a company called Pramukh Films. I tried to trace that company but was unable to find it.'

The first draft of 'Kashmakash' was intensely personal. Guru Dutt poured his disillusionment, disappointment and resentment into the story and promised himself that he'll bring it on screen.

This story would later become his most celebrated film *Pyaasa*. His dream film.

Section Four

DESTRUCTION OF A DREAM

1956–57: BOMBAY

'I'm becoming blind, I can't see.'

12

FIRST SUICIDE ATTEMPT

'I knew he was in turmoil. They had serious problems.'

—Lalitha Lajmi

Just when Guru Dutt's dream project *Pyaasa* was nearing completion, came the news that he had attempted suicide.

'His first attempt at suicide was during *Pyaasa*. It might have been a result of a particularly bad skirmish with Geeta or because he was at an emotional low,'[27] shared close friend and confidant, Abrar Albvi.

It was the year 1956 when the thirty-one-year-old Guru Dutt had swallowed a copious amount of opium. Lalitha remembered, 'I knew he was in turmoil. They had serious problems. He called me and said "Baat karni hai." But when I went, he wouldn't say a word. When the news came we were stunned. We rushed to Pali Hill. I remember his body had turned cold and his vision had blurred. He kept repeating, "I'm becoming blind, I can't see." We took him to the hospital. He was saved.' But what had gone wrong in his life? The artist who had undergone so much struggle to become a winner in life, why did he want to take his own life? The people close to Guru Dutt could never really know if the attempt to end his life was due to a mood disorder, philosophical reasons or just poor impulse control. Neither did they seek professional help after he was discharged from the hospital. The suicide attempt, however, definitely shocked everyone.

But when exactly did his state deteriorate to such an extent that death seemed like the only option? He surely had seen worse days in his life. Then why now, when his art had been recognised and awarded?

With scarce conversations around a socially stigmatised topic and big money riding on his dream project *Pyaasa*, Guru Dutt found little time to address what happened. After the pain he and his family went through, they possibly accepted the common yet highly inaccurate belief that it was on impulse and people who survive a painful suicide attempt are unlikely to try again.

In fact, more often than not, just the opposite is true.

Reportedly, a previous suicide attempt is among the strongest predictors of future suicide attempts. But no one close to him really wanted to contemplate if Guru would ever try to end his life again.

The rejection of the world and life itself was a prominent theme of *Pyaasa.* Drawing inspiration and reliving every trial and tribulation in his life for the script, Guru Dutt literally put his soul into the film. The unfading memory of the *Pyaasa* song 'Ye duniya agar mil bhi jaaye to kya hai', which had Guru Dutt in a posture that symbolises crucifixion is haunting to say the least, as markedly his state of mind was never the same after *Pyaasa*. It was as if the characters of his stories and real life merged into one.

The original title of the story that became *Pyaasa*—'Kashmakash'—also appears in a very important verse by lyricist Sahir. In the film it describes the poet's frustration with the events happening in his life. But looking back, it can be said that the verse also applies to Guru Dutt's state of mind in those days. It was as if his soul was bared.

Tang aa chuke hain kashmakash-e-zindagi se hum
(I am weary of this troubled life, weary of this troubled existence)

Thukra na dein jahaan ko kahin be-dili se hum
(In my grief, may I not reject the entire world?)

Hum gham zadaa hai laayein kahaan se khushi ke geet
(How can I sing of joy when I live in pain?)

Denge wo hi jo paayenge is zindagi se hum
(I can only return to life what life itself offers me)

And then, as if following the strain 'Thukra na dein jahaan ko kahin be-dili se hum' (In my grief, may I not reject the entire world?) Guru Dutt had done the unthinkable.

13

A STAR IS BORN

'It is sad and unfortunate that he never got the recognition he deserved. Neither the media nor the industry gave him recognition then.'

—Arun Dutt (Guru Dutt's son)

On 22 February 1957, *Pyaasa* was premiered at Bombay's Minerva theatre. The leading personalities of the film industry attended the premier.

Within a week of its release *Pyaasa* was much talked about. The humane theme of *Pyaasa* connected with audiences and the film struck gold at the box office. *Pyaasa* scored silver jubilees at many places and even in a non-Hindi/Urdu speaking centre like Madras it ran for fifteen weeks. The media there wrote that the people down south identified their own poet Bharati's life with the story depicted in the film. The commercial success of *Pyaasa* went far beyond Guru Dutt's own expectations. Guru Dutt was elated with the success of *Pyaasa*. He said in a *Screen* interview: 'The success of *Pyaasa* is the best reward of my career. The theme was heavy and I was not all sure that audiences would like it.'

Pyaasa was a revelation. No one had expected such an intense and serious film from Guru Dutt who was dabbling in romantic comedies and thrillers until then. It is to be said that the lyrical fluidity of *Pyaasa* defies Guru Dutt's indecisiveness or temperamental and erratic ways of shooting. The film even today flows effortlessly.

Prof. Ira Bhaskar, the Dean of School of Arts and Aesthetics at the Jawaharlal Nehru University, Delhi says that he was influenced by Hollywood melodramatist Douglas Sirk. Sirk produced highly stylised melodramas. His films had strong women characters. Sirk wrote, directed and acted in his movies and was critical of the soicety and capitalism.

Citizen Kane was a huge influence on Guru Dutt and so was the drama of Orsen Welles. Also, the influence of German expressionist cinema. The entire noir tradition. But equally, and this is not emphasised enough, Guru Dutt was deeply influenced by Indian traditions and Bhakti poetry.

Guru Dutt's inspiration also came from 1940s Indian cinema, works which deeply influenced him. It's not one director or two directors but the Bengali cinema and Bombay cinema of the 1940s. People like P.C. Barua and later Gyaan Mukherjee, who was his mentor.

The year 1957 proved to be a landmark year for Hindi cinema. It witnessed the release of atleast three films which have achieved classic status over the years: Mehboob Khan's *Mother India*, B.R. Chopra's *Naya Daur* and Guru Dutt's *Pyaasa*. Though entirely different in their plots and treatment, the three films shared some common traits. They were deeply rooted in Indian values. More importantly, in all three films moral dilemmas and important social issues were beautifully merged with entertainment, melodrama and wonderful music to produce 'artistic commercial films' with universal appeal. Perhaps that's the reason that even after more than sixty years they don't feel jaded.

Unfortunately, *Pyaasa* did not win any of the prestigious Filmfare awards for 1957. The award ceremony was dominated by *Naya Daur* and *Mother India*. But *Pyaasa* stood the test of time and went on to capture a place in *TIME* magazine's coveted list of 'All-TIME 100 Movies', and has achieved the status of a cult film the world over.

His son Arun Dutt says, 'The biggest irony is he never won any awards. He never canvassed for awards. He never cared about them. Awards had a lot of politics behind them. He never wanted to be surrounded by that kind of politics. It is sad and unfortunate that he never got the recognition he deserved. Neither the media nor the industry gave him recognition then. Many reviews of his films were nasty too.'

Pyaasa propelled Guru Dutt into the league of filmmakers to watch out for. But with *Pyaasa*, another new star was born.

Her name was Waheeda Rehman.

14

THE GIRL WHO CALLED A SPADE A SPADE

'You don't shout at me like this, otherwise I will quit, I can't face it.'

—Waheeda Rehman to Guru Dutt

Waheeda recalled, 'My acting in *C.I.D.* was not good and my work done on the very first set of *Pyaasa* was also disappointing. Everybody said that I was a wrong choice and had no future. Moreover, I was a difficult person, also extremely stubborn, who would not put on this or that dress. But the only one person who seemed to have faith in my abilities was Guru Ji. But for him I would not have been what I am today. After hearing the remarks of everybody he said only one thing, "Let us try her once again".'

There was a spark in the actress that Guru's eyes had seen when he had met her in Hyderabad for the first time. He had become her mentor. Since she came to work in *C.I.D.*, it was Waheeda's clarity and attitude that had struck Guru Dutt. A young South Indian girl without any support in the much vilified Bombay film industry of the 1950s, she must have felt vulnerable. But despite being a newcomer, she drew a clear line and nobody was allowed to cross it. She held her fort bravely and Guru Dutt admired that from day one.

Waheeda Rahman remembered an incident, 'Both *C.I.D.* and *Pyaasa* were being shot simultaneously at Kardar Studios, and he advised me to come and sit on the sets and watch the shooting when I had nothing else to do. One day I saw him losing his temper on a senior artist and I was really shocked. That day I told him, "You don't shout at me like this, otherwise I will quit, I can't face it".'

Guru Dutt was the boss there. No one had spoken with Guru Dutt in that tone.

'I have told you I won't lose my temper with you. Now don't worry,' replied Guru Dutt. Waheeda didn't stop. 'Yes, you better don't,' she insisted and explained, 'I don't know acting. You teach me, tell me what to do and I will try to do my best; but don't get angry with me.'

Guru Dutt just looked at her without saying anything.

'He did not get angry with me, even in the most trying circumstances,' said Waheeda.

Waheeda Rehman said, 'He used to be very impatient, not with the artistes, but with the technicians—especially the camera crew. "Jaldi karo, jaldi karo yaar, abhi tak shot kyon nahin ready hua?" [he would keep saying.] He was always in a hurry because he was constantly thinking about the next shot, the next scene, the next movie. We often told him that you've just given the instructions, it has to take some time to execute them, be patient. But he used to be very restless.'

Remembering the shooting of a song Rahman said, 'The shot of *Pyaasa*, when I come running down the staircase and speak a dialogue was taken twenty times, and every time I failed. By the time I came running down the staircase I was too exhausted to speak the dialogue. He noticed it, came and told me that I should take rest for some time, but I was not prepared to admit that I was tired and the shot could not be okayed till lunch break. But he did not seem to be angry at all. After lunch I had to give fourteen more takes till the thirty-fourth take was okayed. Perhaps a record for me; and also a record of the patience of Guru Ji.'

Guru Dutt also had this peculiar habit of showing the film to close friends and the members of his team. It included the spotboys, to peons, to the biggest actors working in the team. Waheeda Rehman remembered that after showing the film he would ask everyone, 'What do you think about it?' Abrar Sahib used to ask him, 'Why are you asking the valet? What does he know?' Guru Dutt would say, 'No, he's one of the audiences. So don't say that.'

This habit of Guru Dutt led to the removal of a song on Waheeda's suggestion. *Pyaasa* had a song called 'Roop tere' filmed on Waheeda. It came at the point when she gets the news of Vijay's death. The song was shot on a boat in Calcutta. It was a good number but during the trial show of the scenes, Guru Dutt asked Waheeda and her mother about it. Waheeda recalled, 'I said, "The song sounds really nice but it looks very boring." S.D. Burman, the song composer said, "Waheeda, is it really a bad song?" I told him that it was a beautiful song. He asked me, "Why is it boring?" I told him, "According to me dada, this picture is based on the hero, not anybody else. His character has to be highlighted. Now the news has come that he has died, and she is sitting here and crying and singing. It's dragging the script too much."'

Mala Sinha told Waheeda, 'You are a newcomer, you are cutting out your own song?' She said, 'It's so boring! I wouldn't want to watch it.'

S.D. Burman got upset and angry over Waheeda's comment. Guru Dutt just became quiet and later the song was removed from the film.

After the release of *Pyaasa*, Guru Dutt called Waheeda's mother. 'He spoke to my mother,' she said. 'By then he had started to call her Mummy. "Mummy, I want to tell you something. What you mother and daughter were after, cutting out the song, we cut that out." She said, "Oh Guru Dutt, I'm so sorry, we didn't mean to create any problems. We don't know anything about film-making."

Guru Dutt said, "No, you were right. Only the two of you were right."'[28]

15

ARRIVAL OF THE STAR-JODI

> 'The first few years of our married life were happy. But things began getting messy the day Waheeda stepped into the studio.'
>
> —Geeta Dutt

'*Pyaasa* made Waheeda Rehman a star in the Hindi film industry. In fact, the songs picturised on her had made the most impact and were much talked about. The seductive strains of 'Jaane kya tune kahi' and the romantic yearning of 'Aaj sajan mohe ang laga lo', were both in singer (and Guru Dutt's wife) Geeta Dutt's magical voice.

It is true that Geeta Dutt sang at her best during this period. In Hindi cinema, the star actors are often known for their successful songs. The songs they perform to on screen are mostly sung by playback singers but they ultimately become known for the stars they are filmed on.

In a way, the songs sung by Geeta contributed immensely to Waheeda's stardom during her initial years in the Bombay film industry. By then Geeta's own stardom had begun to comparatively fade and she was largely talked about only for the films made by her husband.

'For her part, Geeta Dutt had never taken to Waheeda Rehman. Even if, with a touch of supreme irony, it was Geeta's inimitable style of singing that had witnessed Waheeda Rehman arriving as a heroine opposite Guru Dutt in *Pyaasa*,' writes film music historian Raju Bharatan.

Geeta Dutt told a family friend,[29] 'The first few years of our married life were happy. But things began getting messy the day Waheeda stepped into the studio.'

In 1958, few months after the release of *Pyaasa*, Guru Dutt played the lead role in a crime thriller *12 O'Clock*. The lead actress was, of course, Waheeda Rehman.

Guru Dutt plays a flamboyant lawyer who is out to clear his girlfriend of a murder charge when the evidence points against her. This film is not talked about much as this wasn't officially a 'Guru Dutt film'. It was directed by Pramod Chakravorty who had assisted Raj Khosla on *C.I.D.* Pramod was also Geeta Dutt's brother-in-law (married to her sister, Laxmi Roy). The film was the debut of Pramod as a director and Dev Anand was supposed to play the lead role. But when he couldn't do the film, Guru Dutt stepped in.

With Guru Dutt as the hero, most of the regulars from his A-team perhaps came as a package. The credit roll included the names Abrar Alvi, V.K. Murthy, actors

Rehman, Johnny Walker and Waheeda Rehman. The music was composed by O.P. Nayyar and lyrics were by Majrooh Sultanpuri. Of the seven songs in the film, Geeta Dutt sang five. Three of these were solos and the other two were duets. The album boasts of the fabulous 'Kaisa jaadoo balam tu ne daara' and the romantic chartbuster 'Tum jo hue mere humsafar, raste badal gaye'.

The mainstream masala thriller did average business and was soon forgotten. However, Guru Dutt and Waheeda Rehman's fabulous chemistry was much written about. They were being referred to as the hit star-jodi.

But while this was happening, Geeta Dutt too, wanted her stardom back.

Section Five

BUILDING OF A DREAM

1947–53: BOMBAY

'Apne pe bharosa hai to ek daanv laga le…'

16

GEETA: THE TRUMPCARD

BOMBAY, 1950

'He would listen to one of Geeta's songs over and over again "*Tumi jodi bolo bhalobasha dite janina*" ("If you tell me I don't know how to love")...he was in love.'

—Lalitha Lajmi

When Geeta Roy met Guru Dutt she was a top billing artist and star singer.

Geeta Roy was born on 23 November 1930, as Geeta Ghosh Roy Chowdhary, one of ten children in a zamindar family based in Faridpur, Bangladesh. In 1942, during the Quit India Movement, her family had left East Bengal to settle in Bombay. The family went through a difficult financial crunch and had to struggle even to pay for her singing classes. In 1947, S.D. Burman, who had heard her sing previously, contacted her and gave Geeta Roy her first hit song—the melancholic 'Mera sundar sapna beet gaya'.[30] Geeta was all of fifteen years old at that time. She hadn't seen much life, but there was an innate pain in her voice.

The young girl won countrywide acclaim and in the next two years she managed to overshadow Shamshad Begum and Raj Kumari—the famous voices of that era. Her beautiful voice had an instant connect with the listeners as she moved away from the ghazal style of singing and brought in a fresh spontaneity to her songs. In her own words, her singing sought to give expression to her inner self. Many successful songs followed. She sang in around twelve movies in 1948 and atleast twenty-five films in 1949. She worked with some of the top music directors, including Anil Biswas, Husnlal & Bhagatram, C. Ramchandra, Naushad, Vinod, Ghulam Mohammed, Gyan Dutt, Hansraj Behl, Krishna Dayal, Bulo C. Rani, and S.D. Burman.

After struggling to find work for about a year, a twenty-three-year-old Guru Dutt became an assistant director for the film *Girls School* (1949) and then joined director Gyan Mukherjee on *Sangram,* a crime thriller produced by Bombay Talkies. Director Gyan Mukherjee was a big name in commercial films. He was the man who had directed the most successful film of Hindi cinema at that point of time titled *Kismet,* which ran for nearly five years in a theatre. He became a real mentor for Guru Dutt in the film industry.

Gyan had a huge collection of books and Guru Dutt was allowed to borrow books from his personal library. Working with this mainstream film-maker, Guru also imbibed his technique, commercial aspect of film-making and his flamboyant style.[31]

Though the film business in the Bombay film industry was dominated by Urdu-speaking Punjabis, there were few Bengali teams comprising superb creative talents. Guru Dutt felt more at home in their company. Having spent his formative years in Calcutta, he had a strong affinity towards Bengal, its people and its culture. In an industry where Yusuf Khan became Dilip Kumar and Mumtaz Jahan became Madhubala, he decided to stop using his family name too. Guru Dutt Shivshankar Padukone was now known as Guru Dutt. 'Dutt' was a common surname in Bengal and many in the film industry assumed that he was a Bengali too. Guru Dutt had no problem with it.

Bengal was going to shape his cinema and his life.

Guru Dutt's friend, actor Dev Anand, had become a star riding on the success of his 1948 release *Ziddi*. With his elder brother Chetan Anand, Dev launched his own production company 'Navketan' in 1949. It was now time for Dev to fulfill the promise that he made to his friend Guru Dutt. 'I'm not a promise breaker,' said Dev. Though

Guru Dutt had never directed a film, Dev Anand decided to gamble on his friend from the days of struggle. He asked Guru Dutt to direct Navketan's second production in 1950.

The film was *Baazi*.

'One evening, he returned home laden with gifts and the news that he was directing a film. He told my mother that Dev Anand remembered his promise. We have never seen him so happy,' recalls Lalitha. The time had come for Guru Dutt.

S.D. Burman was composing the music for *Baazi* and he brought on board Geeta Roy as the lead female playback singer.

Geeta writes, '[S.D. Burman] sent word to me that morning to report for rehearsal at the Famous Cine Laboratory and Studios at Mahalaxmi. My father and I drove to the studio and parked the car in the compound. He got out, saying he would inquire where the rehearsals were being held, while I sat in the car. A few minutes later, a young man came up and said, "Come. I'll take you to the rehearsal room." He spoke Bengali, and I took him for one. Not knowing who he was, however, I was a little reluctant to go until his manner reassured me.'

They went upstairs to where S.D. Burman was rehearsing, and at the first available opportunity, Geeta pointed out the young man and asked, 'Who is the Bengali gentleman?' S.D. Burman laughed. 'He's not a Bengali! But his name is Guru Dutt. He is the director of *Baazi*. Don't you know him?'

And so Geeta Roy and Guru Dutt were introduced to each other.

A struggling film-maker and a star singer. This was a story straight out of a fairy tale.

They met again at one of the regular weekend parties organised at Dev Anand's house. These were lovely evenings with guests mingling, laughing, dancing, drinking and eating. During once such evening, Guru Dutt was sitting in a corner quietly enjoying the evening and observing... and then he saw her—the famous singer Geeta Roy. Geeta was talking to Dev Anand. Guru was completely bowled over by her presence.

Guru's eyes met her gaze. He had heard Geeta's honeyed voice, but now he was struck by her beauty. 'She was exquisite like an Ajanta fresco, dark and beautiful!'[32] Lalitha remembered. They smiled, spoke to each other in Bengali. 'My brother had a soft spot for Bengali songs...he would listen to one of Geeta's songs over and over again. "Tumi jodi bolo bhalobasha dite janona" ("If you tell me I don't know how to love")...he was in love.' It was an instant attraction between polar opposites. The extroverted Geeta had reciprocated the feelings of the brooding, introverted Guru Dutt.

Guru Dutt was still about to begin the shooting of his first film, Geeta Roy was already a celebrated singer. Those days she travelled in a limousine. Guru Dutt in buses and local trains. Dev remembered, 'Guru Dutt would travel by buses and trains to pick me up from my home in Pali Hill and take me to his place in Matunga. His mother would take us into her kitchen, make chapattis and serve us food.'[33]

Geeta would also now often drop in at the Matunga house. She was a star but her humility impressed Guru and his family. She would help his mother in the kitchen and won their hearts by her charm and behaviour. Vasanthi became her 'Mashima' (aunt). Lalitha recalls, 'We all loved her. Lovely, wonderful Bengali lady. She used to come in a big car but she was very humble, very good at heart. Whenever she didn't have a song recording, she would come, help in the kitchen too. My mother became close to her. They used to converse in Bangla. Geeta and I used to talk in Hindi.'

Geeta's personality was so charming that the entire Padukone family took to her easily. Lalitha looked up to her as a sister. 'My brother and Geeta were truly in love. One night, I was walking her home when Guru Dutt slipped a letter to me for her. All through their courtship days, I was their courier and chaperone,' Lalitha remembers. They took the little Lalitha wherever they went. They'd exchange letters through Lalitha. Sometimes Geeta would get her car and they drove to Powai Lake, Lonavala and Khandala. Raj Khosla, who was an assistant to Guru Dutt would also often accompany them. There's a smile on Lalitha's face remembering those days, 'It was a very small flat. There was no privacy for them so we would often go to Powai Lake for picnics. Geeta and Guru were very fond of fishing. They would sit silently, fishing for hours. Those visits and long drives I would never forget. Those were memorable and perhaps the happiest days in Guru's life.'

The shooting of *Baazi* commenced and Guru Dutt's professional and personal lives began to take a great turn, but hc had little inkling of the trajectory his life would take.

17

BADRUDDIN JAMALUDDIN KAZI

'It was not that Johnny Walker and Guru Dutt spent several decades together. It was a close, intense association of just ten years. But it was like a lifetime. *Us daur mein rishtey nibhaye jaate the*.'

—Nasir Kazi (Johnny Walker's son)

To create magic on reel, one needs a dream team in real. With *Baazi,* Guru Dutt got a chance to work with people who went on to become his A-team, who were an integral part of many of his memorable films in the next decade.

Dev Anand's elder brother, filmmaker Chetan Anand, wasn't happy with the choice of Guru Dutt as the director of *Baazi*. But Dev Anand was adamant and to prove his point he made sure that each department of the film should boast of stellar talent. Chetan wasn't directly associated with the film but the story of *Baazi* was written by his close friend, actor Balraj Sahni, who was also an active member of IPTA.[34] Zohra Sehgal was asked to choreograph the dance sequences. S.D. Burman was the music composer while the brilliant poet, Sahir Ludhianvi, was writing the lyrics. A very young Raj Khosla, who later became one of the most successful filmmakers of the Hindi film industry, was the assistant director to Guru Dutt.

And then there was Badruddin Jamaluddin Kazi, who we now know as the simple funnyman of Hindi cinema—Johnny Walker.

Badruddin Jamaluddin Kazi was born in 1924 in Indore. His father was a mill worker. The mill closed down and the family moved to Bombay for a livelihood. With his parents and many siblings, Badruddin spent his childhood in utter penury. As a teenager, he sold ice cream, stationery and vegetables to support his family. He mingled with the poor and downtrodden and they formed the core of his golden-hearted, down-to-earth characters. Despite the struggle, life had given him a unique talent for making everyone around him smile. Finally he got a job as a bus conductor with BEST (The Bombay Electric Supply & Transport, its official name until 1995, a civic transport and electricity provider public body). But he wasn't your usual serious bus conductor.

Badruddin turned his profession into an art.

While issuing the tickets and during the bus journey, he took it upon himself to entertain the passengers with funny anecdotes, jokes and calling out bus stops in a way that would make everyone laugh.

One such evening, it was actor Balraj Sahni travelling in the bus when Badruddin's 'show' was on. Balraj was amused at the conductor who had made the bus into his performance stage. He was hugely impressed with the young man. Sahni was writing *Baazi* and asked Badruddin to meet Guru Dutt for a 'surprise' audition. The surprise meant that Badruddin would perform without Guru Dutt being informed.

And so it happened.

Guru Dutt and Dev Anand were in the midst of discussing a scene on the sets of *Baazi*. Suddenly a 'drunkard' turned up tripping over every little thing. There was sudden chaos on the sets. All eyes were on the funny drunkard who was uttering strange gibberish. His antics amused Guru Dutt and Dev Anand and they started laughing. The unit members got hold of the man. But suddenly the man straightened up and said in a soft voice that he was not drunk. Guru Dutt was fascinated. The talent of Badruddin and his impromptu audition had definitely impressed him. He was now going to be a part of *Baazi*.

Nasir recalled an interesting anecdote that his father shared with him from the early days. Guru Dutt asked. 'What should be your name in the credit roll? Should we write Badruddin Qazi?' The reply came, 'Aisa lagega main nikah padhaane ja raha hoon kisi ka.[35] Also, eveyone will come and tell my father, "Qazi sahab ka beta actor ban gaya."[36] Please think of some other name for me.' Guru Dutt said, 'You act phenomenally as a drunk man. My favourite whiskey is Johnny Walker. So Johnny Walker it would be.'

The film credits him by his real name, Badruddin. But inspired by his act and based on Guru Dutt's favourite whiskey brand, Badruddin Jamaluddin Kazi was rechristened as Johnny Walker. Ironically, he had never even touched alcohol in his life.

If Guru Dutt placed his faith in an artist, he would give them a lot of room. Johnny Walker said, 'He'd tell us, "Johnny, ye tumhaara scene hai, ye dialogue hai, ye shot hai. Isme tum jo behtar kar sakte ho to karo."[37] That's what he would say, then off I'd go. In each rehearsal, I'd say some lines extempore. In every rehearsal, I would come up with something new. Guru Dutt used to love that. He used to look at everyone on the sets, and see if the light-boys, the cameraman, the assistants, were laughing at my dialogues. Guru Dutt had an assistant write down whatever I said in the rehearsals. That's how we worked. The reason I did so well in all of Guru Dutt's films was that I had found the man who knew how to draw out my talent, otherwise it would have stayed within me.' Johnny Walker didn't receive much formal education but was an eager student of life. While Guru was impulsive, Johnny, in real life, was a serious, wise man who never forgot Guru's contribution and friendship. Guru Dutt too respected his talent and earthy wisdom.

'Dono ki technically shuruaat to ek saath hi hui thi,'[38] said Nasir. 'Or we can say that their first success was together through *Baazi*. They became close friends. They helped each other professionally. Us daur mein rishtey nibhaye jaate the.[39] That's why the bond was so strong. There used to be fights, arguments between Guru and Johnny and the rest of the close-knit team for a scene, for a script…these arguments used to be phenomenal. Guru Dutt allowed such discussions. But the following day after the arguments everything was fine again,' remembers Nasir.

It was a friendship and an association that would indeed last for a lifetime.

18

RAJ KHOSLA

'We would sit together, he wouldn't speak for hours…but I could never touch the core of his heart.'

—Raj Khosla on Guru Dutt[40]

Born on 31 May 1925, Raj Khosla initially entered the film industry with hopes of making it as a playback singer. Struggling to make it as a singer, he joined Guru Dutt instead as an assistant director with *Baazi* (1951), thanks to the film's producer/actor, Dev Anand. He went on to become one of the top directors, producers and screenwriters in Hindi films from the 1950s to the 1980s. He was also the man behind the success of *Baazi* which proved pivotal for the risk-taking appetite of Guru Dutt and ultimately gave birth to *Pyaasa*.

Raj Khosla explained Guru Dutt's approach, 'Guru Dutt's interest in detail was tremendous…what worried him was: "What is my artist thinking at the moment in the story?" I miss his quietness. We would sit together, he wouldn't speak for hours...but I could never touch the core of his heart. He was deeply affectionate to everyone, to servants, and the humblest man. He was devoted but could not express his love. You see it's one thing to love someone but it's another to express love. So the whole thing came out in his films. That love he put through his movies.'

The story of *Baazi* was about Madan (Dev Anand), an out-of-work taxi driver who falls for the proverbial 'fallen woman' with a golden heart, Neena (Geeta Bali), who reciprocates his love. There was also a 'Hitchcockian appearance' of Guru Dutt in the opening shots of *Baazi* where he plays the role of a poor man smoking—a precursor to his days as a full-fledged actor.

Guru Dutt shared the story credit with Balraj Sahni in the film's credits but during the making, Balraj was unhappy with Guru Dutt's style of working. Their worldview and vision could not match. Balraj, a staunch leftist, was an active member of IPTA and for him films were meant to spread social ideas and messages about equality and justice. Guru Dutt belonged to the Gyan Mukherjee school of filmmaking and wanted to make commercial films. He was interested in dances, songs and mainstream elements to make a successful and entertaining film rather than 'teach' the audience something. In his autobiography,[41] Sahni has written about how Guru Dutt's sense of script was weak. While Sahni felt that screenplay was the most important element of a movie, Guru Dutt focused more on song sequences that were to become his signature in Hindi cinema.

Dev Anand had to often play the peacemaker during heated arguments between the director and the scriptwriter. At Guru Dutt's Matunga flat, they had many sessions discussing the screenplay. But when the shooting of *Baazi* began, Balraj Sahni was also shooting for a film called *Hulchul*. So he was not always physically present on the sets of *Baazi*. He was upset when he realised that the screenplay had been changed by Guru Dutt.

They never worked together again.

But the gamble paid off. *Baazi* was a smash hit with its high entertainment value. Guru Dutt, who till now was a hitherto unknown assistant director, overnight was catapulted into the big league. The success of *Baazi* had also ended Guru Dutt's financial struggle. He bought the first ceiling-fan for the family flat and a radio, which the family kept as a memento for years. 'There was a time when he couldn't attend a shooting schedule because he had only two pairs of trousers: one was dirty and the other was at the laundry,' Lalitha said. Guru also asked his mother to leave her job at the school as she had 'toiled and sacrificed enough' for the family and it was time for her to relax.

Baazi had truly changed lives.

Baazi was also a landmark film in Dev Anand's career. Till then he had given some successful films that belonged to social, comedy or romantic genres but *Baazi* gave him a brand new screen persona with grey shades which was starkly different from his previous clean-cut, cute-looking roles. The cap, the cigarette and the styling did wonders for Dev's projection as the rebellious romantic star. In his autobiography,[42] Dev Anand wrote: '*Baazi* gave me an image that stayed in the minds of people, and made a genuine star out of me. For the first time I felt and saw what stardom was in terms of adulation and fan following. I became a phenomenon after the release of *Baazi*.'

Guru and Dev Anand had fulfilled the old promise they had made to each other.

19

V.K. MURTHY

'From the next film onwards you will be my cameraman, we will work together.'

—Guru Dutt to assistant cameraman V.K. Murthy

Baazi became a milestone in the short-lived genre that can be loosely called Bombay Noir. Though Guru Dutt is best known for his serious social 'message' films like *Pyaasa*, he was also an early pioneer of the Bombay Noir genre, with films like *Jaal, Aar Paar* and *C.I.D.* 'The cinematography is dark but while much of the style is borrowed from Hollywood's caper and crime films, Bombay Noir as practised in India also had songs, a comedy track and "Indian" emotions,' says writer and film historian, Siddharth Bhatia.[43]

Guru Dutt had discovered a template for urban crime thrillers. *Baazi* could also be seen as a precursor of his later films that had a similar emotional core. The central characters in his later films varied from a taxi driver, a poet, a film-maker to a servant, yet each one had similar world views dealing with melancholy and loneliness—good-hearted men/artists losing their innocence in the big bad modern world.

But more than anything else, it was Guru Dutt's innate talent of song picturisation that surprised everyone. Songs and dances have always been an integral part of Indian cinema but Guru Dutt gave them his own unique touch. It was really his phenomenal craft of song picturisation that has contributed the most to his greatness as an illustrious filmmaker.

At a time when songs were used merely as 'items' or musical breaks to divert the attention from weak scripts, Guru Dutt began using them as an extension of the script rather than as random interval points. As a result, the songs did not appear as mere standalone musical pieces but deeply integrated into the plot and often took the story forward. The song 'Suno gajar kya gaaye' has the vamp warning the hero to be careful as there's a danger to his life. Or the character of Geeta Bali seamlessly breaking into the song 'Tadbeer se bigdi hui taqdeer bana le' to console her lover Dev Anand who is going through emotional turmoil and needs to take a critical decision.

Guru Dutt's signature style was also to begin a song without the introductory music. So a character would talk and then break into a song without a prelude or introductory music, making the song an extension of the dialogue.

In Hindi cinema, the script is usually interspersed with songs that usually follow a similar language, irrespective of the tone and form of the script or the socio-economic background or language of the character singing the song in the movie. For example, a hero playing a criminal would suddenly break into a romantic song. Guru Dutt rejected that format. It was important for him to stick to the 'vocabulary of his characters' even in the songs. He even shot many songs on outdoor locations, at places that his characters were supposed to inhabit, against the norms of song picturisations on tacky indoor 'sets'.

Right from his first film *Baazi,* despite limited resources, his focus was on the brilliant picturisation of songs. His childhood passion of creating images with light and shadows remained an integral part of his film-making. Combined with his learnings of dance and drama at Uday Shankar's dance centre in Almora, Guru Dutt was going to take the use of light and shadows to an almost poetic level in his cinema.

Guru had realised a band needed more than a vocalist to create music. He wanted a team of artists as passionate as him who could understand his language of cinema. On the sets of *Baazi,* Guru Dutt recognised one such person with whom he was going to create unforgettable images and emotions on screen.

His name was V.K. Murthy.

Born in Mysore, Venkatarama Pandit Krishnamurthy or V.K. Murthy, learned music and trained as a violinist in school. An angry teenager, he was even jailed in 1943 for participating in a protest during the Indian freedom struggle. Later, he completed his diploma in cinematography and came to Mumbai to pursue a career in the visual medium. But neither music, nor his anger left him. Working with his closest associate, Guru Dutt, he was to create emotions through his camera—images that were lyrical, haunting, disturbing and unforgettable.

Guru Dutt was shooting for *Baazi* when he met Murthy, who was then assisting the cinematographer V. Ratra. Realising that the debutant director was open to creative suggestions, Murthy offered advice to shoot an important sequence in the song. In the film, the shot has the camera panning from a reflection in the mirror to Dev Anand and then on to the floor of a club where Geeta Bali and her chorus girls are dancing to 'Suno gajar kya gaye'. Murthy had already thought about how the music could be complemented with camera movements. He told Guru Dutt, 'If you don't mind, I could suggest one thing; see there is a big mirror, we can use that to create a great sense of movement.' Dutt asked, 'How?' Murthy said, 'Put the camera on the mirror and make Dev Anand start here from his reflection. I will move the camera as he walks towards it to the dance. I will follow him until he goes and sits on the chair.' The camera used to have a dolly. Murthy placed the camera according to the music and rehearsed the timings. By now he had also realised that Guru Dutt was a very short-tempered person on sets. So he said, 'Look Guru Dutt, I will take three or four takes and I will tell you which is good, and you have to keep the take that I approve.' He agreed to this. The second take was okayed.

Guru Dutt was delighted. That evening after the shooting had packed up, Guru Dutt walked up to Murthy and said, 'From the next film onwards you will be my cameraman, we will work together.'

The process of building 'Team Guru Dutt' had begun.

20

LOVE AND LONGING IN BOMBAY

'*Apne pe bharosa hai to ek daanv laga le...*'

—Geeta Dutt's song in *Baazi*

The high point of *Baazi* was a superb musical score by S.D. Burman dominated by singer Geeta Roy who sang six solos out of the eight songs. While every song in the film created stir, it was 'Tadbeer se bigdi hui taqdeer bana le' that stood out for its innovativeness and effortless charm. Sahir had written a ghazal which was innovatively set to music in the western style by S.D. Burman. With Geeta, he had given a new expression to 'seductive club songs' which used to be very popular in those days.

The film media was writing extensively about how Geeta Roy's voice has contributed tremendously to the thundering success of boyfriend Guru Dutt's first film. She was flooded with offers of singing in big films, travelling and performing in Kolkata, Hyderabad, Madras and London.

Most of the reviews were cruel but *Baazi's* high entertainment value made it a success at the box office.

Baburao Patel in his negative review called the film 'poorly directed' with a 'badly handled story'. Grapevine even hinted at the new director on the block riding on the success and status of the star singer Geeta Roy.

Geeta Roy's family didn't care much for Guru Dutt. For them, Guru Dutt was only a struggler and belonged to a different community. But Geeta was drawn towards Guru. Whenever she didn't have a recording, she'd drop in at his house. She could play the harmonium with ease and often sang her songs steeped in emotions, reminiscent of Bengali culture, 'Mera sunder sapna beet gaya' (*Do Bhai*) and those from *Jogan*.

Guru Dutt's family doted on her. Geeta became very close to Lalitha. 'Those were such happy days. Raj and Geeta used to sing the song "Khayalon mein kisike" from *Bawre Nain* (1950). Geeta was close to me too and would even sing songs on the phone to me. She was a star. I remember one full moon night in the balcony of her bungalow at Amiya Kutir[44] she confided, "I'm going to marry your brother!" I was elated,' said Lalitha.

The family though, was very worried about Guru Dutt's short temper and lack of communication skills. At times, it was difficult to figure out his moods. Guru Dutt mostly remained quiet. He would hardly show his emotions and usually stayed away from the glamour and glitz while the extroverted Geeta loved meeting people and partying.

But both loved their drink…and rain.

Bombay rains usually come without a warning. When it rains in Bombay, it pours. But whatever Guru and Geeta were doing, they couldn't resist rain. They would leave evrything and simply head out on the road.

Guru would say, 'Let's go! It's raining I can't work now. Can't stay at home in such beautiful weather.'

With Geeta by his side, he drove slowly on the highway with raindrops falling on the car. The drizzles, the liquid sunshine and Geeta singing Guru Dutt's favourite songs. Truly blissful. 'Raj Khosla and I would pile on and we'd go for long drives, usually to the wonderfully secluded Powai Lake. Raj and I made sure the couple in love had some time together,' recalled Lalitha.

In those moments they truly felt 'made for each other'.

But like Bombay rains, their clashes also came without a warning. The occasional fights between the couple used to make Vasanthi worry for their future together. She tried to seriously raise the issue with Guru Dutt. They had these conversations about the inherent differences in their personalities. But finally Guru Dutt replied, 'Ma, you know I love Geeta. I am a person who never breaks my promise. I have given her the promise. No one can change me. After all, it is one's destiny.'

21

THE WEDDING

> 'Geeta-Guru event came to be portrayed as one of the most romantic weddings in filmdom. Made for each other looked the two.'
>
> —Raju Bharatan

As soon as Geeta's family got hint of her closeness to Guru and his family, they began objecting. She was the primary earning member of the family and a star. They didn't want to lose her. Often her brothers would come to Guru Dutt's home looking for her. Lalitha says, 'If they found her she would say she had come to meet her friend Lalli (Lalitha). They had a close Bengali family friend who they had in mind for Geeta, and they hoped she would be engaged to him soon.'

Guru Dutt's mother writes, 'Guru was furious when he heard that Geeta had another friend, who was a Bengali… Guru and Geeta used to have misunderstandings and she would not visit us for days together. Guru Dutt would get upset. He would come home late at night, worried and mentally disturbed. He never spoke to anybody.'

Guru Dutt had earlier been in two relationships that hadn't worked out and had left him heartbroken. He met her parents and tried to convince them but they just put off the matter. Lalitha reminisces, 'Geeta could be moody…after one of her arguments with my brother she had disappeared for days. She went off to a friend's place in Bhusawal without telling anyone. Guru Dutt was worried out of his mind.'

He now became insecure and wanted to get engaged to Geeta and put an end to their regular squabbles. Guru realised that her family favoured the Bengali boy for Geeta. This troubled him deeply. Perhaps thoughts of the previous broken relationships also troubled him. He wasn't able to concentrate on work so he decided to have a final conversation with Geeta.

It was a rainy day when Guru Dutt took Geeta to the Haji Malang shrine. It's the tomb of a saint on a high hill in Kalyan, thirty miles away from Bombay. Devotees believe if a person prays at the Haji Malang dargah, their wishes get fulfilled. Guru Dutt had deep faith for this place. Whenever he was dealing with crisis, he would visit the shrine. Vasanthi writes, 'Guru Dutt asked Geeta to make up her mind, either to choose him or the Bengali boy and not play with his sentiments. She chose Guru Dutt.'

Together they persuaded Geeta's family for the engagement. In 1952, the grand ceremony was finally held at Poddar College in Matunga. Guru Dutt and Geeta Roy were finally engaged to be married. Meanwhile, he had shifted to an apartment called Sunder Villa in the Bombay suburb of Khar with his mother, sister Lalitha and brothers, Devi Dutt and Vijay. His father, Shivshankar Padukone, and brother, Atmaram, stayed on in the Matunga flat. The family was happy about the Guru-Geeta engagement and wanted them to marry soon.

It was the evening of 26 May 1953. After three years of being engaged, Guru Dutt and Geeta Roy decided to get married. The wedding ceremony was performed at Geeta's mother's home, Amiya Kutir, in Santa Cruz, Bombay. It was a traditional Bengali style wedding. That morning some of Geeta's close friends went to Guru Dutt's flat on 12th Road, Khar with chandan[45] paste and garlands. He was dressed in a white silk kurta and dhoti worn in the Bengali style. Bridegroom Guru Dutt Padukone arrived in a tastefully decorated Hudson convertible.

Geeta looked ethereal as the young bride. 'She was around twenty-one and made for a beautiful bride in a red Banarasi sari with a thin red veil and lots of gold jewellery.'

The wedding conducted according to Bengali rites was a glitzy affair. It was attended by many well-known personalities of the film industry, including Dev Anand and elder brother Chetan Anand, Nutan, Vyjayanthimala, Geeta Bali, Kalpana Kartik (set to wed Dev Anand), Nalini Jaywant, Ramanand Sagar, Kamini Kaushal and Sumitra Devi. Guru Dutt's family had never seen such a grand wedding function in their family. His mother remembered, 'With great pomp the wedding took place! It was the film industry's sensation at the time.'

The singing icons were there in full force too: Lata Mangeshkar, Talat Mahmood, Mohd Rafi, Hemant Kumar and Kishore Kumar. The best part of the reception was Guru Dutt's chief assistant director, Raj Khosla, had persuaded each one of the top singers there to render something—with the condition that the song *had* to be from a Guru Dutt movie. And such was their love for Geeta that they all obliged. The only orchestral support for the singers was the 'recurring bow-wow-wow of Guru Dutt's inseparable dog, Tony'.

Those days Talat Mahmood always sang last as the one billed to be a star performer. He crooned the freshly put out Majrooh Sultanpuri ghazal: 'Mujhe dekho hasrat ki tasveer hoon main.'

'I remember how this Geeta-Guru event came to be portrayed as one of the most romantic weddings in filmdom. Made for each other looked the two,' wrote Raju Bharatan.

Late at night, with the music of shehnai and the sound of conch shells reverberating in the background, the couple took seven rounds around the holy fire—the Saptapadi ceremony.

Guru Dutt and Geeta Roy were finally man and wife.

'I welcomed my first daughter-in-law by performing the "Bou-Bhaat" ceremony according to our customs...I prayed to god for their long life, prosperity, health and happiness,' recalled Vasanthi.

Geeta was very close to Guru's sister Lalitha Lajmi, 'I didn't call her Bhabhi. I used to address her as Geeta. She was very generous and loving. She used to tell me, "Open my cupboard and pull out whichever sari you want to wear." Once I told her I'd never travelled in a plane. She flew me to Delhi for a show, where we stayed at the Imperial hotel. It was through her that I got a chance to meet legends like O.P. Nayyar, Lata Mangeshkar, Majrooh Sultanpuri and Sahir.'

In Guru Dutt's family, Geeta was the star.

At the time of the wedding, Geeta was more popular and making more money than Guru Dutt. The press, film industry gossip as well as the relatives were insinuating that Guru Dutt had married Geeta for her money and fame. These rumours reached Guru Dutt's family. Though the sensitive Guru Dutt never reacted to it, his mother wrote, 'The public as well as the relatives were saying that Guru Dutt married Geeta because of her wealth and her big name in the industry…Guru Dutt never had any yearning for wealth. I think he never even glanced at her jewellery. Inspite of his earlier hardships he never wanted to hoard money. He had already bought a two-seater sports car for himself. He would not interfere with Geeta's earnings, nor would he ask how she spent her money.' People who knew Guru Dutt closely were of the view that Guru truly wasn't into money. For him money meant nothing more than a commodity to trade dreams with.

'Between Geeta and Guru, it had been decided before marriage that his wife would be still actively singing after their wedding—something in which she was flourishing. As a career woman, Geeta was accustomed to making her decisions by herself, being a singer in recurring demand. Whatever the equations at home, the picture of cooperation was Geeta at the mike,' wrote Raju Bharatan.

But despite these hurtful gossips Guru and Geeta were in the happiest phase of their life together. 'We met for the first time during the making of *Baazi* and it was three years later, during the making of *Baaz*, that we were married. From *Baazi* to *Baaz* it was just a matter of dropping the "I"—and converting it into a "We",' wrote Geeta Dutt.

The star-singer Geeta Roy had now changed her surname and went by the name Geeta Dutt.

But as life unfolded, she realised it wasn't just the name that had changed.

Section Six

DESTRUCTION OF A DREAM

1953–58: BOMBAY

'Don't make this film, it's just your personal life.'

22

REEL VS REAL

'Though I stop Geeta from singing, I still want her to be famous.'

—Guru Dutt

'Somehow, I had an intuition that Guru and Geeta's marriage would never be a happy one. Firstly, in those days, she earned in thousands whereas Guru's income was limited compared to hers. Secondly, both were stubborn, would never yield to one another. Thirdly, Guru had a burden of responsibilities over his shoulders,' said Guru Dutt's mother, Vasanthi.

There was a strange paradox in Guru Dutt's approach to his cinema and his personal life. In films, he talked about 'working women' and breaking of useless traditions, while in his personal life, he demanded adherence to 'traditional' values of marriage and motherhood. (This hypocrisy was also evident in his films like *Baaz* and *Mr. & Mrs. '55* where independent women gave up everything for their love.)

Perhaps a career-oriented and ambitious wife was not what he had imagined despite knowing that Geeta was the star when they got together. Guru Dutt's mother wrote, 'Guru Dutt could not tolerate women drinking heavily. In certain ways he was old fashioned. He disliked parties and the so-called women's lib. He was Indian at heart. In this way, Guru Dutt and Geeta were losing each other. It was so pathetic to observe. But, no one had the boldness to bring them together.'

The equation between them had now completely changed.

In the book *Binidra*, writer Bimal Mitra recalls this conversation he had with Guru Dutt,

'Why do you stop Geeta from singing?' once asked close friend and writer Bimal Mitra[46] to Guru Dutt.

Guru Dutt was startled. Then he composed himself and said, 'Geeta has told you this?' He paused, then after a thought resumed, 'Bimal Da, when I married Geeta she was a star singer. But slowly, her career waned. Now, her name doesn't carry the same glamour.'

'Why do you say that?' Mitra questioned.

'Arrey! Does any one person's glamour last forever?' said Guru Dutt.

'Ok, glamour is one thing but her singing is still respected. She has a lot of offers,' weighed in Mitra.

'I know there are offers but her fame is not like it used to be. When an artist is on the downslide, the artist should pause. He should be silent.'

'But any artist cannot remain at the top forever. That doesn't mean Geeta should completely stop singing,' Bimal Mitra argued.

It was then that Guru Dutt accepted that he doesn't want a singing career for Geeta. He said, 'Listen, though I stop her from singing, I still want her to be famous.'

'No, you just don't want her to be *more* famous,' said Mitra.

'What are you saying? I never had such thoughts,' said a baffled Guru.

'It's possible you don't want to think about it but deep down this is your thought process. When you got married to Geeta, she was more famous than you. Now you are more famous. Geeta thinks that you are responsible for her downfall,' said Mitra.

It was as if Bimal Mitra had touched a raw nerve. Guru Dutt was silent for a few moments.

Then he said, 'But I let her do playback in all my films.'

'So?' asked Mitra. 'You think you become great by doing that?'

Unfortunately, there is little in the public domain from Geeta's point of view. The author and music critic, Raju

Bharatan, recalls a conversation with Geeta Dutt, 'She was understandably bitter about her "continuing to sing" being resented. She said she had made a few things clear to one and all even before her marriage. She had emphasised how her work would entail late hours almost daily. All the more so as she took on songs in not so high-grade movies. Such songs got recorded only in cheaper second shifts (3.00 to 9.00 PM with the rare evening possibility of one-hour overtime). At one stage it was even suggested that with growing kids to look after, Geeta should be singing only in Guru Dutt movies. This, said Geeta, would have virtually meant her singing for "the one and only...", referring to Waheeda Rehman.'

From *C.I.D.* onwards, every movie that came out of Guru Dutt Movies Pvt. Ltd. starred Waheeda Rehman in the lead role—the 'one and only' female lead actor for his films. So by default, Geeta ended up being the 'voice' of Waheeda in some of the finest song sequences in Indian cinema. There was much being said about the on-screen chemistry between Guru Dutt and Waheeda Rehman and the off-screen gossip was reaching Geeta's ears too.

Lalitha Lajmi says, '...Geeta was suspicious by nature. She was extremely possessive. That's a huge let-down in any marriage and created major problems in their relationship. A filmamaker or an actor works with many actresses. For the film, they have to express love on screen and make it look real. But Geeta couldn't accept this after their wedding.'

Geeta Dutt had a circle of Bengali friends that included Hemen Gupta and his wife; singer-music composer Hemant

Kumar and his wife; and, Manna Ladda, the distributor from Bengal. But the closest friend of Geeta was Smriti Biswas, the actress who played an important role in the flop film *Sailaab*. The group partied hard regularly but Guru Dutt excused himself from those get-togethers.

According to Abrar Alvi, Guru Dutt did not like Smriti Biswas and thought of her as a bad influence on Geeta.

Remembering Geeta Dutt, Smriti Biswas said, 'Geeta was "saawali"[47] but so beautiful! She had a beautiful voice. But yes, she was suspicious and possessive. It wasn't her weakness, it was her nature…Guru and Geeta loved each other a lot. But a creative person wants space. He couldn't handle the possessiveness. When Geeta pestered him for attention, he'd say in jest, "Bore mat karo."'[48]

Smriti also said that she often helped good friend Geeta Dutt keep a tab on Guru Dutt's whereabouts. This particularly led to a very unfortunate incident a year later from which the Guru-Geeta relationship never really recovered.

Guru Dutt's mother writes, 'Geeta was by nature jealous and temperamental. Her so-called well-wishers provoked her by exaggerating the studio news. She used to pay attention to such people. Thus, the misunderstanding between Guru Dutt and Geeta increased. Guru Dutt's sensitive mind was always distressed. He would convince Geeta about the real position. But she ignored his words.'

Raju Bharatan wrote, 'One reason for the two never "agreeing to differ" could have been that Geeta was as unyeilding, by disposition, as Guru Dutt. Not enough give and take? Who really knows in a marriage gone wrong?'

23

BIRTH OF AN ACTRESS

1957

'Why do you keep saying Waheeda-Waheeda? I can also be a heroine. Am I any less good-looking than Waheeda?'

—Writer Nabendu Ghosh quoting Geeta Dutt

Geeta was getting anxious and irritable. She was often lonely because Guru never communicated his feelings and emotions and had also started spending too much time in office. Lalitha says, 'Guru Dutt was a workaholic. Nothing mattered except work. Also when he was upset he would go quiet. He would never share what's going on in his mind.'

Various people close to Guru Dutt have time and again repeated how his off-camera communication skills were exceedingly poor. The trials and tribulations of the finances and responsibilities of running a production house and his own film banner was weighing down on him—something the artist in him had little experience in.

More than loneliness, it was the feeling of worthlessness that had also taken over Geeta. Unable to reconcile with her personal and professional frustrations, she found solace in liquor.

Sensing that Geeta was drifting away and to mend their relationship, the thirty-two-year-old Guru Dutt, on his first overseas trip to West Asia/Europe, called Geeta to Beirut for a holiday together.

From Beirut, Guru Dutt wrote a letter to his mother:

> Dearest Ma,
>
> I am writing this from Beirut. It is a beautiful place. But inspite of everything I miss home, Geeta and you all. I wish I had brought Geeta along with me. The other day I had phoned Guruswamy to arrange for her coming.

Geeta soon reached Beirut. During their stay in Beirut, Guru Dutt discovered a new market for Indian films and met the famous composer, Abdul Wahab. Guru Dutt recounted, 'I asked him to write the music for one of my forthcoming films, which I propose to make in Arabic and Hindi. In order to prove my bonafides I said I would show him a few reel of my pictures, which I had taken along. But it was not necessary. Abdul Wahab said: "Your manners have convinced me that you are an artist. I will write the music for your film."'

In Beirut, Mehboob Productions' *Aan* starring Dilip Kumar had an uninterrupted run of several weeks while in Tehran, Guru Dutt saw a poster of the film *Dhoon* which starred Raj Kapoor and Nargis as the former's films were very popular in Iran.

In Rome, Guru Dutt visited the famous Cinecitta Studios which was a huge establishment—bigger than a dozen Bombay studios put together. Though Guru Dutt found them to be the same as Indians when it came to shooting and dialogue delivery.

Arriving in Paris, Geeta was mobbed everywhere they went. People gathered around her, admiring her multi-coloured sari or her features. In London, a musical function was organised by the Asian Film Society and Geeta was the star of the evening. Although the audience there did not understand the Hindi language, they seemed to enjoy Geeta's singing. 'Music has no geographical frontiers,' observed Guru Dutt.

It was during this trip that a major decision was taken to not just revive Geeta's career but to launch her as an actress too.

No one knew this would soon lead to the unmaking of Guru and Geeta's relationship.

Right after their return, Guru Dutt announced his next movie *Gouri* with Geeta Dutt in the lead role. She was to be launched as a singer-actress. The film was to be made in Bengali and English.

Nabendu Ghosh—the famous Bengali author and screenwriter, who wrote classic films like *Bandini*, *Devdas*, *Abhimaan* and *Teesri Kasam*—had written the story of

Aar Paar for Guru Dutt previously. He writes in his autobiography *Eka Naukar Jatri* (Journey of a Lonesome Boat), 'I got a call from Guru Dutt once again. I went. Dutt said, "Nabendu Babu, I am making a Bengali film this time." I remembered his grasp over the Bengali language and said, "You have that right so it's good news." "Then write me the screenplay," he said.'

He further writes that it was a touching story and he agreed to do its screenplay. 'Who would star in it? The hero, of course, would be Guru Dutt, and the heroine would be his beautiful wife Geeta. Because one day she had told her husband: "Why do you keep saying Waheeda-Waheeda? I can also be a heroine. Am I any less good-looking than Waheeda?" Her words had touched Guru Dutt so he decided Geeta would be the heroine of the film *Gouri*.'

True to his style Guru Dutt visioned a grandiose cinematic spectacle. He decided that *Gouri* would be the first CinemaScope film of India. He wrote to 20th Century Fox in Hollywood to create the anamorphic lenses for the CinemaScope format. With the new anamorphic lenses, he asked cinematographer V.K. Murthy to film some test shots of Geeta Dutt. Murthy filmed Geeta sitting on a swing in the garden of their Pali Hill bungalow.

The film became the talk of the town.

Geeta was excited to play her part as the singer and debutant actress in *Gouri*. Music composer S.D. Burman had composed and recorded two songs for the film. Things had started looking sunny again. *Gouri* was going to be the grand comeback Geeta had been waiting for. A renewed hope of a new beginning in her life and career.

But hope, sometimes, is a dangerous thing. It has the potential to ruin you.

Gouri was being made to resurrect the damaged relationship of Guru and Geeta. But what happened during the shooting of *Gouri* changed their lives forever.

Guru Dutt planned an outdoor shooting schedule for *Gouri* in Calcutta. A huge house was rented in the New Alipore area and his entire unit was staying there. Even though it was a Bangla film, Guru Dutt was spending money like it was a big-budget Hindi film. While making a film, he never cared about how much money was being spent. Only the quality mattered. He shot on many locations: farms, forests, rivers and roads. Kolkata-based National Award-winning director, Nripen Ganguly, recalled,[49] 'Dutt had shot extensively in Kolkata in quite a few locations. I was there on the day when he was filming the immersion scene on the banks of the Ganges. Geeta Dutt was present during the shooting.'

After the shoot, the unit used to come back to the New Alipore house but Guru used to go to watch the rush prints. He used to watch the rushes till late night. Then again he'd be shooting the next morning. During the shoot of his films, he was like a man possessed.

As a director, Guru Dutt had his own vision of presenting his lead character, Gouri, while Geeta looked at it differently. Outside the sets, Guru Dutt was a friend, a sensitive listener, a lover, a father or a husband. But on his film sets he was just a stubborn artist. A ruthless dictatorial director who would not listen or agree with anyone easily, even if the lead actress was his own wife.

For him, Geeta was just an actress and that's where the problems began.

The shooting went on for a few days and then came the storm.

Gouri was destined to doom. So were Guru and Geeta Dutt.

24

THE UN-MAKING OF *GOURI*

'Tum kya chahte ho...yahi na ki main Waheeda Rahman se badtar lagoon?[50]

—Geeta Dutt to Guru Dutt

One morning of the shoot schedule in Calcutta, the crew were preparing for the shoot to begin.

'The shot is ready! Call Geeta!' Guru Dutt said.

The assistant replied, 'She is doing her make-up. Will take some time.'

For the scene, she had to wear an old worn-out sari with her hair untied and a bindi on her forehead. Guru Dutt didn't want too much make-up on her. *Gouri* was a tragic love story about a sculptor of Durga idols (played by Guru Dutt) who falls in love with a prostitute Gouri (played by Geeta). Guru Dutt wanted her to look the part.

Everyone waited for a while. An impatient Guru Dutt now asked Ramu Saria to go and bring Geeta from the make-up room.

Distributor Ramu Saria was based in Calcutta and Guru Dutt had invited him to the shooting location.[51]

Here's how writer Bimal Mitra narrates the incident in *Binidra*:

> When Ramu reached he saw Geeta was fixing her hair.
>
> 'Bhabhi, everyone is waiting. The shot is ready,' he said.
>
> 'Bas Bhaiya…coming,' said Geeta.
>
> Ramu Sariya kept waiting. Some more time passed. Geeta continued working on her hair and make-up. Guru Dutt was getting irritated. He decided to go and call Geeta himself.
>
> As soon as he looked at Geeta, he was shocked.
>
> 'What have you done?' he shouted in anger. 'Who asked you to do this make-up?'"

In his mind, Guru Dutt had conceived a certain image of the character of Gouri. It was conveyed to Geeta during the discussion of the script. As a director, any digression from that image was non-negotiable for Guru Dutt. But in this case the equation was more complicated. The lead actress was his wife and their relationship was going through a challenging phase. Was this a husband shouting at his wife? Or an artist shouting at his subject for the sake of art?

'I told you the character will appear in "simple" makeup. There would be no overdoing of style. And this hairstyle? Do village girls have such a hairstyle?' Guru kept shouting in anger in front of many people from the unit.

There was shock and disbelief on Geeta's face. Finally, she shouted back, 'Tum kya chahte ho…yahi na ki main Waheeda Rahman se badtar lagoon?'

For a few moments there was a pindrop silence. Then Guru Dutt turned around and shouted, 'Pack up! Pack up!' Then he left immediately. Ramu Saria also left with him. He turned his car towards a bar in Chowringhee.

Two days later the entire unit left Calcutta. Back in Bombay, the gossip columns were on full display.

The writer of *Gouri*, Nabendu Ghosh, writes in his autobiography *Eka Naukar Jatri*:

> 'Guru Dutt went to Calcutta with his whole team and shot for almost three months but suddenly returned to Bombay without finishing the film. Why? Why? Why? This "Gouri" got drowned in the water that flowed out of the eyes of a beautiful woman—who was this beautiful woman?
>
> A voice whispered, "Waheeda Rahman", the heroine of Guru Dutt's company.'

25

GEETA, INTERRUPTED

'Suddenly, no one knew what happened. Geeta refused to work in the film…Guru Dutt was completely broken by the shock of having to discontinue the film.'

—Vasanthi, Guru Dutt's mother

There are multiple versions behind the shelving of *Gouri* but Guru Dutt himself had a conversation about it with close friend and famous Bengali writer Bimal Mitra.

'Geeta was the lead actress in the film. But there was some reason why I didn't complete it,' Said Guru

'Why? Why didn't you complete it?' asked Bimal Mitra.

'Because of Geeta,' replied Guru.

'But Geeta told me you stopped the film for some other reason,' confessed Bimal.

'What did she tell you?' said a surprised Guru.

Finally, Bimal Mitra dropped the bomb. 'Geeta said it was because of Waheeda Rahman.'

Guru Dutt's eyes and face turned red. He clearly denied that Waheeda Rahman had anything to do with the shelving of *Gouri*. He told Bimal Mitra, 'Do you think I wasted lakhs of rupees on the film for no reason? For years I had wished to make a Bengali film. But Geeta herself thwarted my wish.'

Recalling the crucial incident Guru Dutt's mother later wrote, 'Suddenly, no one knew what happened. Geeta refused to work in the film…Guru Dutt was completely broken by the shock of having to discontinue the film. For one week he disappeared and no one could trace him.'[52] Guru Dutt's sister Lalitha Lajmi assigned it to 'ego problems' and said, 'Geeta had some problems during the shooting in Calcutta. Their relationship was going through a very bad phase. Geeta had some ego problems due to which the film was later shelved.'

Guru Dutt later said, 'I shelved the film because of Geeta…Geeta wasn't listening to me. When I am directing a film, I am not a husband or a son, I am only the director of the film.'

Filmmaker Nripen Ganguly who witnessed the shooting of *Gouri* said, 'We had heard that this film was shot to repair the relationship. But, that didn't happen and the film was abandoned.'[53]

Unfortunately, there's no version from Geeta in the public domain. She never talked about *Gouri* in her interviews.

Though in Guru Dutt's filmography, *Gouri* is mentioned only as a shelved film, but it truly had a devastating effect on his personal life.

Author Raju Bharatan remembers a conversation with actress Uma Anand, who also co-wrote the film *Taxi Driver*. Uma had seen Guru Dutt grow up professionally in front of her eyes from his formative 1950–51 *Baazi* days at Navketan Films; she had been married to Chetan Anand at that point of time. Raju Bharatan writes, 'Guru Dutt Shivshankar Padukone would fly into an uncontrollable rage. That would create immense problems for wife Geeta Dutt who was still absolutely stable herself—who, in fact, was endeavouring to put her sadly interrupted singing career back on track.'

The shelving of the film *Gouri* had a severe impact on both, but Geeta was particularly devastated. There were reports of complaints from music directors about her not being easily available for either rehearsals or recordings. She neglected her riaz.[54] Around the same time, S.D. Burman fell out with Lata Mangeshkar. He could have made Geeta Dutt his main singer rather than the upcoming Asha Bhosle but that did not happen. Geeta, reportedly, owing to a disturbed personal life, was not able to practice sufficiently and couln't focus on her work. It was reported that she failed to meet the quality expectations of S.D. Burman who was a hard taskmaster. This was one of the reasons why S.D. Burman and later O.P. Nayyar turned to Asha Bhosle.

Lalitha Lajmi recalls, 'Slowly, stories about Geeta's alcoholism were heard. I never saw her drinking openly though. It first began with sleeping tablets. Then it went on to some kind of drugs…[55] Lalitha Lajmi told this author it wasn't just Geeta, both of them took to drinking heavily and consuming sleeping pills. Sleeping pills were the new fad in those days.'

The thirty-three-year-old Guru Dutt's downward emotional spiral too was triggered after the collapse of *Gouri*—the first to-be CinemaScope film of India, the first to-be Bengali film of Guru Dutt, the first to-be film to launch Geeta Dutt as an actor, but it only ended up as the first unfinished, abandoned, shelved big budget project of Guru Dutt.

The marriage was not working yet their intense love for each other often came to the fore. In a letter to Geeta dated 28 July 1958,[56] Guru Dutt writes: 'Darling, whatever may happen remember you are a part of me and you will always be a part of me. Perhaps you may not know how much I love you. Perhaps when I am no more then you will realise.'

It had only been six years since Guru and Geeta had together dreamt and worked to set up the Guru Dutt Films banner while working for other producers in films like *Jaal* and *Baaz*.

They could have never foreseen the demolition of that dream.

Section Seven

BUILDING OF A DREAM

1953–55: BOMBAY

'What is the secret of this frenzy?
From where does it come?'

26

GURU, THE LEAD ACTOR

'I said you look like a hero, why do you want other people to act as heroes in your films?'

—V.K. Murthy

To understand the demolition, one first needs to understand the hard work that went into the building of the dream. The process of building 'Team Guru Dutt' was completed in his next two films: *Jaal* and *Baaz*. It also led to the beginning of a new journey for Guru Dutt—as a lead actor.

Released in September 1952, *Jaal* wasn't as big a commercial success as *Baazi* (1951), though it won praise for Guru Dutt for his slick direction. As a director *Jaal* became Guru Dutt's last film with Dev Anand. According to Raj Khosla, Dev was steeped in his mannerisms while Guru Dutt wanted his performances to be more realistic. It wasn't easy to force Dev Anand, the star. There were instances when Guru Dutt used to get irritated. But they were close friends. A headstrong Guru Dutt decided that he would become an actor to portray his characters as he had visualised them.

Off-screen, Guru Dutt was a poor communicator. His brother Atma Ram who was also his assistant in *Jaal* said, 'He was a very hard taskmaster and very dedicated to his work. On the sets it was difficult to say what was on his mind. He tended to keep everything to himself and wouldn't communicate with the assistants, which made things rather difficult. So he shouted a lot. Often he used to set the shot by looking through the view-finder and develop his ideas visually, which would become confusing to us, and even to the artists. He never told the artists in advance what to do. He would make them stand in a particular frame and then develop the idea of the shot through the view-finder. Often I would be the stand-in for some artists and there would be [a] lot of shouting. But looking back on his films one realises what a fine visual sense he had. The film is essentially a visual medium. And he was trying to communicate to the audience visually first, in his brilliant way. That was Guru Dutt's strength.'[57]

Veteran film producer and lyricist, Amit Khanna, who worked closely with Dev Anand for many years says, 'Many times Dev Saab and Raj Khosla used to talk about Guru Dutt. Dev Anand remembered fondly how he and Guru would go together to watch English films. He said Guru

Dutt believed strongly in the popular appeal of cinema. Commercial success of his films was really important for him.'

Though it is often said that Guru Dutt was a reluctant actor but some people suggested that he actually wanted to be talked about as an actor-star. That's the reason that in most of his films, though the first choice of the lead actor used to be someone else, ultimately, he used to cast himself as the hero.

This began with a small appearance in his first film *Baazi*. After *Baazi*, Guru again had a Hitchcockian appearance as an unshaven, shirtless fisherman in the song 'Zor lagake haiya' in *Jaal*. It can be said that during *Jaal* he had started considering the idea of becoming a full-fledged actor. V.K. Murthy said, 'I said you look like a hero, why do you want other people to act as heroes in your films? At first, he didn't agree then I said, "Let me take a screen test, you judge for yourself." So in the first schedule of *Jaal*, when we were shooting an outdoor sequence, I told him, "You come and do this role." It was not an important role, just a fisherman. We did the shoot, he looked at the results and they proved what I had said.'

During the making of *Jaal*, Guru Dutt met S. Guruswamy, the production in-charge, who would become an integral part of all his films starting with *Jaal*.

Guruswamy had earlier worked with the famous Bombay Talkies and a couple of years at Indian National Pictures. In Bombay Talkies, Guruswamy rose to become the production secretary. In 1947, after the death of Bombay Talkies' founder, Himanshu Rai, Guruswamy became the secretary to his wife, the famous Devika Rani. When Devika Rani quit films to marry the Russian painter Roerich, Guruswamy too left in 1949.

'Guruswamy was Guru Dutt's most trusted team member. Guru Dutt met him during the shooting of *Jaal* and they became friends. Later Guru Dutt invited him to join as the production-in-charge in his film company,' says Lalitha Lajmi.

'Guru Dutt gave me great freedom in business dealings, although the final decision would rightly be his,' recalled Guruswamy.

Guru Dutt had directed his two initial films (*Baazi* and *Jaal*) with two different producers. In both the films he was dissatisfied with the interference of the producers. He wanted to produce films himself. But he didn't have enough money. Geeta Bali, the lead actress of both films, offered him a business partnership. In September 1952, Geeta Bali's elder sister Haridarshan Kaur and Guru Dutt formed a new film production company. They named it H.G. Films, taking the initials of the two partners. The first film to be produced by this company was named *Baaz*.[58]

Baaz was a costume drama inspired by western high sea thrillers and a complete misfire and unarguably Guru Dutt's worst film. It is mainly remembered for the fact that this was the first film where Guru Dutt appeared in a lead role. But despite his good looks, his performance as an actor in *Baaz* was unremarkable.

As a director too, he seemed disinterested in the proceedings. Clunky screenplay, ridiculous dialogues and cheap special effects marred Guru Dutt's dream to produce a grand high seas adventure. The huge ship where most of the action takes place was built in an open field behind Shrikant Studio in Chembur. Unfortunately, owing to the juvenile special effects, the boat looked like a toy boat in the movie.

Geeta suggested Guru to work with a then little-known music composer O.P. Nayyar (Onkar Prasad Nayyar). Geeta told Guru that O.P. was a commercially oriented music director and combined with Guru Dutt's sense of song picturisations, the result could be special.

'Geeta Dutt had the most original voice in film music. She was the one who introduced me to Guru Dutt,' recalled O.P. Nayyar.

Geeta was right about Nayyar. *Baaz* witnessed the emergence of a winsome combination of Guru-Geeta and the gifted O.P. Nayyar. Together they were going to create magic.

As a 'debutante lead actor' Guru Dutt was criticised a lot in *Baaz*. This was also to be taken head-on in Guru Dutt's next film.

27

THE MAN WHO GAVE WORDS TO GURU'S ANGST

'I told him that the dialogues of the movie should be according to the character.'

—Abrar Alvi

During the making of *Baaz,* there were major arguments between Dutt and the dialogue writer, Sarshar Sailani. Sarshar followed the heavy theatrical style of writing dialogues in Urdu, a form prevalent in those times, especially for period dramas. Guru Dutt had a very modern outlook when it came to film-making. He believed that writing for screen is different from writing for stage productions. His visual sense and characterisation needed a new form of writing. He wanted a writer whose writing was less loud or verbose and more natural with free flowing humour. He found this gift in writer Abrar Alvi.

After dabbling in theatre, and a stint directing radio plays in Nagpur, Abrar Alvi eventually came to join the Bombay film industry with the help of his cousin, a young actor named Jaswant. This cousin was playing an important role in Guru Dutt's *Baaz* and was dating the co-producer Haridarshan Kaur.

One day after an argument with *Baaz*'s dialogue writer, Sarshar Sailani, Guru Dutt asked his assistant Raj Khosla to re-work on the dialogues for a scene. Abrar was present on the sets accompanying his cousin.

Abrar recalled, 'I loved driving and, therefore, I started going to the shooting of *Baaz* as a driver with Jaswant. I soon became good friends with the film's assistant director Raj Khosla.'[59]

That day when Guru Dutt asked Raj Khosla to work on the dialogues, Raj asked for Abrar Alvi's suggestion. Abrar told him he couldn't suggest how a character would speak till he knew their background, class and education. After Raj explained, Abrar went on to improvise the scene, without realising that Guru Dutt's sharp eyes had already recognised the hidden talent.

Guru Dutt was impressed with Abrar's observations about dialogue writing. He inquired about Abrar, his background and his educational qualifications. A few days later, Guru Dutt called Abrar Alvi home and asked him directly, 'Would you work with me on writing my next film?'

Abrar Alvi told Guru Dutt that he had no experience of screenwriting, and that he had only written plays during his college days. To be fully sure, Guru Dutt tested Abrar for the next one week. He called Abrar home every day and gave him a situation or scene to write. The condition was

Abrar couldn't leave his home and had to write in isolation. Guru Dutt wanted to make sure that Abrar didn't take anyone else's help.

He was building a team and screenwriting was going to be the most important pillar from then on. Whatever Abrar was writing in those seven days, Guru Dutt was discussing that material with other trusted friends and even with his mother. Vasanthi told Guru that she liked Abrar's style of storytelling.

That sealed the deal.

Guru Dutt called Abrar and told him, 'You're going to write my next film,' with a caveat that he will be present on the shooting throughout and would guide the actors in emoting and delivering the dialogues properly. Abrar agreed.

Guru Dutt's mother Vasanthi wrote about this crucial association, 'Guru gave a chance to Abrar Ali in this picture. They became good friends in later years.'

In those moments, neither Abrar nor Guru Dutt had the slightest idea that together they would create a body of work that would stand the test of time for its craft and universal emotions.

28

THE CAMARADERIE OF 'TEAM GURU DUTT'

'He'd sit back and enjoy the verbal sparring like watching two cocks fight. This was one of Guru's favourite pastimes. And Johnny and I always fell for it.'[60]

—Abrar Alvi

Baaz was trashed for every aspect but the reviews were particularly harsh for Guru Dutt's direction and his debut as a lead actor. The review in *Filmfare*[61] said:

> What could have been a good swashbuckling adventure film is here reduced to a comparatively tame picture owing to the inadequate direction and unknowing treatment of an otherwise action-packed story…(The drawing of the Portuguese characters in the film is naively done and shows a conspicuous lack of polish, especially in the direction.)…
>
> Dutt as the hero is not dashing enough, and plays the part too tamely.

Such savage reactions for his work used to hurt Guru Dutt. After making a successful debut with *Baazi*, his graph was on a decline with an average earner *Jaal* and the flop *Baaz*. He wanted acknowledgement as a film-maker. As an actor it made him question his decision to play lead roles. He asked writer Abrar Alvi what he thought of the film (*Baaz*) and his performance in it. Alvi, in an effort to sound evasive, replied, 'Aap bahut photogenic hain [You are very photogenic].' Guru Dutt answered back, 'Kucch actogenic bhi hain ya nahin [Am I also a little actogenic or not].'[62]

The huge failure of *Baaz* and the heavy financial losses incurred by the newly formed company H.G. Films led to Guru Dutt and Haridarshan Kaur going separate ways. Guru Dutt, with the help of Geeta, bought Haridarshan Kaur's share and started his own company: Guru Dutt Films Private Ltd.

The failure had its silver lining too. Guru Dutt was now free to make films of his choice without anyone interfering or dictating the terms. In a way, the 'Guru Dutt cinema' as we know today truly began taking shape post the failure of *Baaz*.

The wedding of Guru and Geeta definitely brought the much needed luck for Guru Dutt. He had already begun working for his next film *Aar Paar*.

Geeta Dutt was closely involved with the casting and

A lobby card of *Kaagaz Ke Phool* (1959). The famous *Kaagaz Ke Phool* (1959) first scene in the studio when the once-famous/now-forgotten filmmaker Suresh Sinha (Guru Dutt) comes to the studio.

Guru Dutt and Shakila in *Aar-Paar* (1954).

---

hotographs courtesy of Lalitha Lajmi's personal collection, National Film Archive of India, Pune

At the Berlin Film Festival for the screening of *Sahib Bibi Aur Ghulam* (1963). Guru Dutt, Waheeda Rehman and Abrar Alvi.

Guru and Waheeda in Berlin. According to Waheeda Rehman, they met in Berlin for the last time. They never worked together after *Sahib Bibi Aur Ghulam* (1963).

Guru Dutt and Abrar Alvi at the premiere of *Pyaasa* (1957).

Waheeda Rehman (Shooting still from *Sahib, Bibi Aur Ghulam*)

Guru Dutt reading some film trade newspaper. Commercial success and business of films was always important for him.

Geeta Dutt with Guru Dutt's mother Vasanthi Padukone.

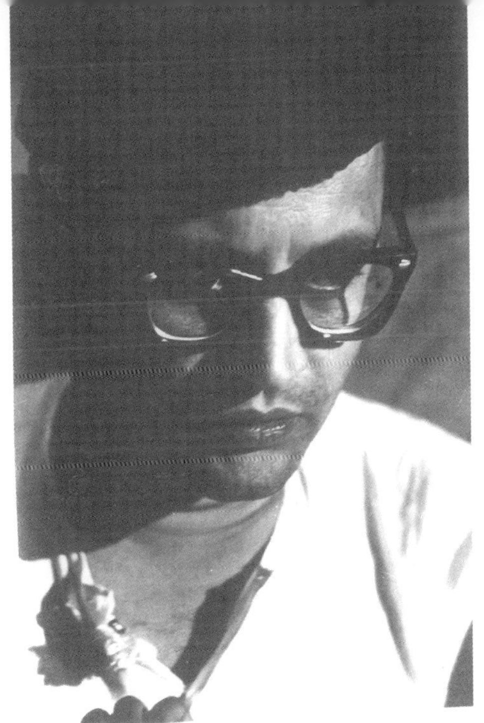

Guru Dutt created magic with his melancholic eyes but very few know that he wore thick glasses in real life (it's possible he couldn't even see the camera lens clearly while emoting).

Guru Dutt with Raj Kapoor. Guru was very impressed with the popularity of Raj Kapoor's films abroad. He wanted to show him his film *Kaagaz Ke Phool* (1959). It could never happen. One of the last few calls he made were to Raj Kapoor.

Guru Dutt in *Pyaasa.*

Guru Dutt's final scene, the film is *Baharen Phir Bhi Aayengi* (1966). Playing a reporter in the film, he resigns from his job. He throws his resignation letter on the table and tells his editor (Mala Sinha), 'Whether you accept it or not, this is my resignation. I am going...'

Guru Dutt with Sarvepalli Radhakrishnan.

Guru and Geeta Dutt, united in matrimony.

Geeta with a young Tarun Dutt, their son.

Guru with Dev Anand and Johnny Walker. Friends for Life.

Postcard/letter he sent to his mother from Beirut.

Guru Dutt and Waheeda Rehman. Shooting still from *Sahib, Bibi Aur Ghulam* (1963).

Geeta Dutt. The star singer who married a struggling film-maker.

Chaudhvin Ka Chand (1960): Guru Dutt's biggest commercial success ever.

Geeta Dutt.

Guru Dutt at his Lonavla farmhouse.

Aar-Paar (1954).

Dev Anand in Guru Dutt's directorial debut, *Baazi* (1951). Fulfilling the promise between them: whoever will make it first will give the other friend a chance.

Guru Dutt with Geeta Bali in *Baaz* (1953), also Dutt's first lead role. A failure at the box office.

Guru Dutt and Waheeda Rehman in *Chaudhvin Ka Chand* (1960).

(Below) Guru Dutt and Waheeda Rehman in *Kaagaz Ke Phool* (1959), India's first CinemaScope film and this one is considered to be an iconic shot for its lighting and composition. Shot inside Mehboob Studios in Bombay.

Kaagaz Ke Phool (1959): The rise of the director.
Fans lining up for autographs. The world at his feet.

(Below) Guru Dutt with Madhubala in *Mr. & Mrs. '55* (1955).

Another wonderful shot from *Kaagaz Ke Phool* (1959) filmed inside Vauhini Studious, Madras.

(Below) The mental asylum scene in *Pyaasa* (1957). A disturbed Guru Dutt often used to tell his friends: 'Mujhe lag raha hai main pagal ho jaoonga.'

A still from the song 'Jaane woh kaise log the' in *Pyaasa* (1957), inspired from the crucification of Christ.

(Below) Waheeda Rehman in her famous song from the Telugu film *Rojulu Marai* (1955).

The ethereal Meena Kumari as Chhoti Bahu in *Sahib Bibi Aur Ghulam* (1963).

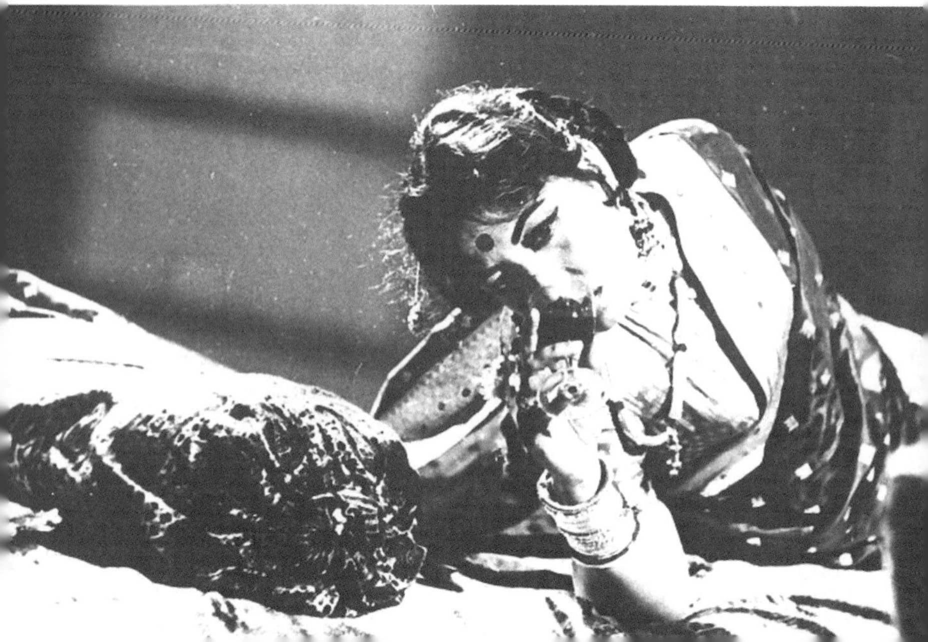

A young Guru Dutt at Uday Shankar's India Cultural Centre in Almora (1942–1944).

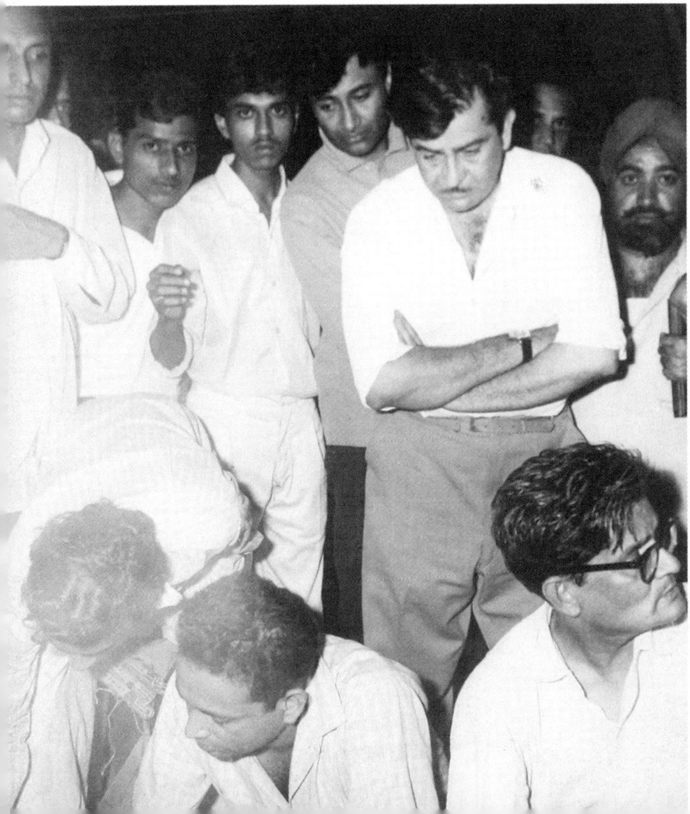

A friend gone too soon. Dev Anand and Raj Kapoor at Guru Dutt's funeral.

Geeta Bali (Guru Dutt's first lead actress) and Geeta Dutt.

(Below) The three tigers. Guru with Guruswamy and Johnny.

The family: Guru and Geeta with Tarun, Arun and Nina.

(Below) Guru and Geeta Dutt.

A young Guru Dutt in Calcutta.

(Below) Sudarshan Benegal, B.B. Benegal, Guru Dutt and another member of the Benegal family.

Guru Dutt with Dev Anand. The close friend from the days of struggle in Poona.

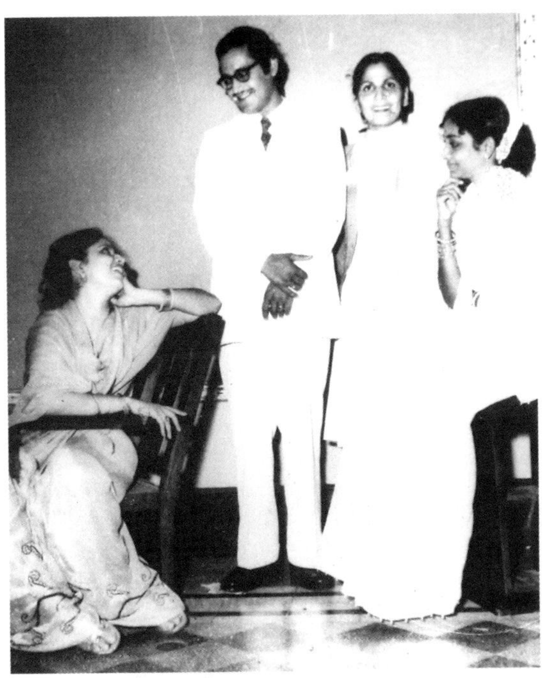

Guru with Geeta Bali and Geeta Dutt.

Guru Dutt with Bimal Roy,
a film-maker he respected a lot.

Credit: Tabeer K. Asif Qureshi and Akbar Asif

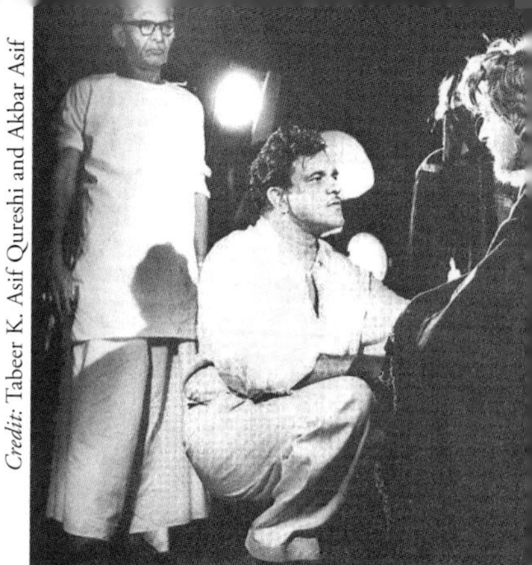

Guru Dutt with K. Asif on
the sets of *Love and God*.

Guru Dutt and Geeta Bali.
Shooting for *Baaz* (1953).

(Below) *C.I.D.* (1956).

Credit: Tabeer K. Asif Qureshi and Akbar Asif

Shooting still from K. Asif's *Love and God*, Guru was playing Majnu in this but died before completing the film. This was supposed to be K. Asif's next mega project after *Mughal-E-Azam*.

Jaal (1952).

(Below) *Pyaasa* (1957).

12 O'Clock (1958).

(Below) Guru Dutt with Sahir Ludhianvi.
The on-screen and off-screen poets of *Pyaasa* (1957).

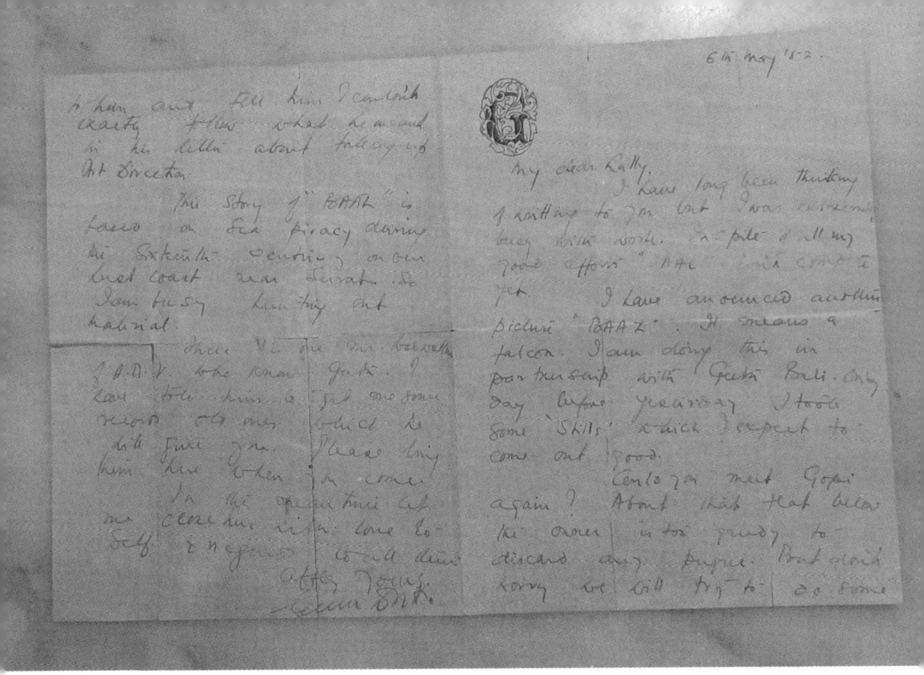

Guru's letter to his sister Lalitha while he was planning to make *Baaz* (1953).

(Below) Guru Dutt and Mala Sinha on the sets of *Baharen Phir Bhi Aayengi* (1966).

The baby Guru Dutt.

(Below) Guru Dutt with Shashi Kapoor, Abrar Alvi and Shammi Kapoor.

Guru in Europe.

(Below) Guru Dutt's letter to his mother.

Amiya Kutir
63, Linking Road
Santa Cruz (West)
Bombay 23.

26. 2. 51

dearest Lali

To day I am feeling little bit alright that's why I am writing to you a letter.

We have not met about a week, really I am missing you very much. And I am geting bored on the bed. When mashiama will be coming from Poona? I hope when I will go to your place — mashiama will be there. Has Atma ram also gone to Poona? How is he? How is Debdas, and Bijay and didima? I am very enxious to see all of you. And I hope I can meet every body very soon.

I think you are very busy with your house works, because you are — incharge of your house now. If I was alright then I could help you a

Geeta Dutt's letter to Lalitha Lajmi.

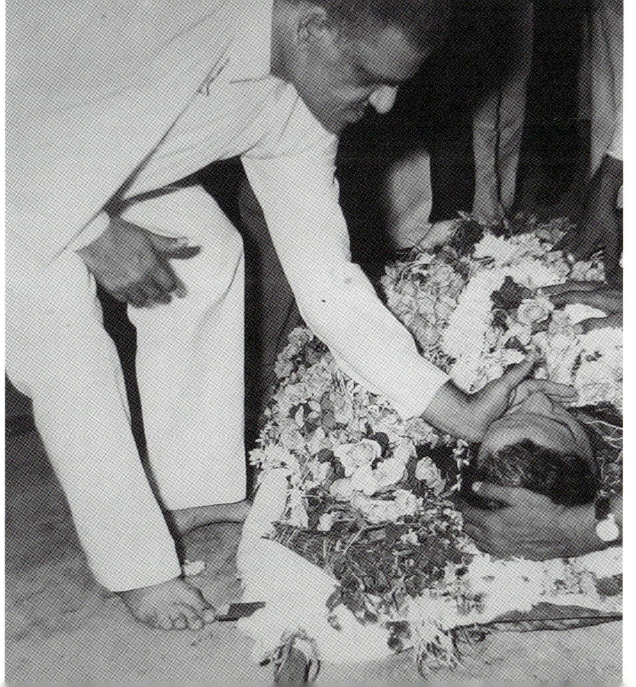

K. Asif paying his last respect to Guru Dutt at his funeral.

Lalitha Lajmi with the author.

the music of the film. Nabendu Ghosh was writing the screenplay and writer Abrar Alvi, the new addition to Team Guru Dutt, was to contribute to the screenplay as well as write the dialogues.

As the lead actor of *Aar Paar*, Guru Dutt gave a confident performance but few know that he had in fact decided to cast Shammi Kapoor for the role after shooting a few reels with himself. In a meeting between them, Shammi keenly watched the scenes with Guru Dutt as the lead actor. Refusing to sign the film, Shammi convinced Guru Dutt that he himself was indeed the best choice for the lead role. Guru Dutt finally took up the challenge and acted with a resurrected confidence after his dismal performance in *Baaz*.

For the lead actress, Shyama's name was suggested by Geeta Dutt. However, Geeta herself was present during the shooting of the romantic scenes. Shyama fondly recalled, 'Guru Dutt was a romantic really, and Geeta was very possessive. She would come to the sets and used to keep an eye on him. That made me laugh.'

In *Aar Paar,* Guru Dutt also gave Johnny Walker a major role as a comedian. Abrar Alvi recalls, 'Johnny Walker had a wonderful sense of humor. I myself was very good at repartee and Johnny could crack jokes. Guru Dutt exploited this weakness by deliberately leading us on to get into acerbic conversations; then he'd sit back and enjoy the verbal sparring like watching two cocks fight. This was one of Guru's favourite pastimes. And Johnny and I always fell for it.'[63]

Guru Dutt liked the simplicity and talent of Johnny Walker. 'So strong became their relationship that he was part of every film Guru Dutt made either as director or as a producer. Except one—*Sahib Bibi Aur Ghulam*—which I directed,' said Abrar Alvi.

Together Guru Dutt, Johnny Walker, Abrar Alvi and Guruswamy would go on hunting expeditions. They worked together, they partied together.

This camaraderie of the team members was translating beautifully on celluloid too.

Aar Paar was a charming film with the crime noir part wonderfully infused with romance and humor. Guru Dutt's character had some of the elements that remained common in most of his lead characters: The hero was an underdog, looked towards society with sarcasm, was shunned by his family but loved by two women. One of the women was the proverbial 'fallen woman'.

Most of Guru Dutt's iconic films have an underlying premise of the 'other woman'. In *Baazi* it was Kalpana vs Geeta Bali, in *Aar Paar*, Shyama vs Shakila, in *C.I.D.*, Shakila vs Waheeda Rahman, *Pyaasa* had Mala Sinha and Waheeda Rahman, *Kaagaz Ke Phool* had the wife and the actress (Waheeda).

This is the film where Guru Dutt seemed in control. As a director, he would lend a freshness to the plot with his innovative framing, pace and superb song picturisations. 'He was a tiger on the set,'[64] recalls his cinematographer V.K. Murthy.

The critics had torn apart his earlier films *Jaal* and *Baaz*. *Aar Paar* changed it all. The encouraging review of *Aar Paar* in *Filmindia* magazine said:

> Guru Dutt however has produced *Aar Paar* with such an accent on entertainment, making the crime content incidental, that the picture does become quite enjoyable with its fast and furious action. Production values are quite good…Photography is quite pleasing and there is a rare sense of harmony in cameraman Murthy's work… Guru Dutt's direction is quite smooth for his limited purpose of entertaining without straining the mind.

V.K. Murthy said, 'He would never compromise on the way the film turned out, the way each scene linked with the other. He was an obsessive director, and until the shot came out just as he wanted he would continue with as many takes as he needed, without a break.' Murthy added, 'He never said "Okay, jaane do".'

29

THE WIZARD OF SONG PICTURISATION

'Many people copy him but he was the first to make the song visually interesting…he'd spend nights thinking of song situations.'

—Majrooh Sultanpuri

The biggest reason behind *Aar Paar*'s success was undoubtedly the O.P. Nayyar-Geeta Dutt combo. Out of the eight chartbusting songs, seven had Geeta Dutt's vocals. Praising Geeta Dutt, O.P. Nayyar said, 'Who will deny there is a unique quality to her singing? Give her a blatantly westernised tune this moment and a complex classical composition the next, and she will do equal justice to both with an ease of expression which a singer can only be born with…Geeta Dutt is an asset to any music director.'

The evergreen song 'Babuji dheere chalna' was inspired from 'Quizás, Quizás, Quizás', written in 1947 by Osvaldo Farrés, a Cuban songwriter settled in New Jersey. Geeta

Dutt created magic with her seductive vocals. Coupled with Guru Dutt's inimitable style of song filming, the seductive cabaret song picturised on Shakila gave a new dimesion to the club songs of those times. Shakila remembered the hard work she had to put in for the songs, 'Guru Dutt was a wonderful person and a perfectionist. In *Aar Paar* I had a song sequence which he wanted me to do in a particular way. He took 30-40 takes before he was satisfied!'

'Hoon abhi main jawan' had Geeta Dutt projecting in her intoxicated voice the deadly mix of vulnerability and seduction. Then there was the vivacious 'Yeh lo main haari piya' picturised in a taxi, in O.P. Nayyar's rhythmic beats. And who can forget the ever romantic 'Sun sun sun sun zalima' sung by Mohd Rafi and Geeta Dutt.

In an interview with author Nasreen Munni Kabir,[65] the lyrics writer Majrooh Sultanpuri narrates an interesting anecdote. Sultanpuri had initially written 'Sun sun sun sun zalima, Pyar mujhko tujhse ho gaya.' But Guru Dutt wanted to change it to 'Pyar humko tumse ho gaya'. Sultanpuri disagreed saying it was grammatically incorrect as you can only say 'tumse' if you use the plural 'suno suno' (not 'sun sun'). Majrooh recalled, 'I still remember the way Guru Dutt said, "Arey yaar, Majrooh, chhodo na, gaana sunne ki cheez hoti hai, itna kaun wahaan tumhara grammar leke baithega?' (Oh come on Majrooh, forget it—a song is a thing to be listened to, who is going to bother about your grammar?) Majrooh had to agree. 'The song was a big hit even though there was a grammatical fault in it,' laughed Majrooh.

Majrooh Sultanpuri further notes, 'Many people copy him but he was the first to make the song visually interesting. His greatest talent was his consistency. His songs were always on a higher level, they had impact. He gave them much thought, he'd spend nights thinking of song situations.' The norm of those times was to picturise songs indoors or on sets, sometimes unconnected to the characters singing the song or their background. But Guru Dutt preferred locations that his characters inhabited in the story—so the 'Kabhi aar kabhi paar' song is not in a park or a romantic setting so typical in the films of those times, but under the scorching sun near a construction site, next to a broken car. The romantic 'Sun sun sun sun zalima' is filmed in a garage with an old car as the main prop. The long tracking shots with smooth camera movements, intelligent play of light and shades, poetic silhouettes and the wonderful use of close-ups, all these were trademark Guru Dutt elements that gave his songs and films a distinct lyrical quality. With *Aar Paar* these hallmarks had started to fall in place.

Another unusual quality in Guru Dutt's songs was that any character could sing in his films. So it wasn't just the lead actors on whom Guru Dutt picturised the songs. In his films, some of the most popular songs feature character actors or even characters who had no connection with the story. So a random construction worker sings the very popular title song of 'Kabhi aar kabhi paar laaga teer-e-nazar'. This character is never seen again in the film. The only non-Geeta Dutt song, it was sung by Shamshad Begum in her usual robust style. And since it was mandatory in a Guru Dutt film to have a song picturised on Johnny Walker, *Aar Paar* had 'Na na na tauba tauba' sung by Mohd Rafi. Johnny Walker's natural flair for comedy combined with Guru Dutt's unorthodox style of song picturisation gave the 'comic relief song' genre a new meaning.

The actress opposite Johnny was Noor, actress Shakila's younger sister. During the shooting, the two fell in love and got married.

Aar Paar was Guru Dutt's second smash hit as a director, first as an independent producer and first as a successful actor. The press was calling Geeta his lucky charm. It was true to a great extent.

Success was a great leveller in the relationship of Guru and Geeta.

30

THE PRICE OF SUCCESS

'Geeta was fond of glamour and publicity. They always differed in their tastes and opinions.'

—Vasanthi, Guru Dutt's mother

Aar Paar's success changed Guru Dutt's status tremendously. Professionally, Guru and Geeta were now offcially a 'superhit team'. There was more good news on the personal front. Geeta and Guru Dutt were expecting their first child. Due to her pregnancy Geeta had reduced her singing assignments.

In the previous four years Lata Mangeshkar had emerged as the new singing sensation with more chart-busters. Though in the initial years, Geeta had shown more versatility. Her inimitable voice sounded ethereal in bhajans, romantic songs, seductive cabaret songs as well as the sad, melancholic numbers. But it was clear that she had been relegated to the number two position, though she and Lata were the top two female playback singers of the 1950s.

Most of her time was dedicated to the family and focusing her energy on Guru Dutt's films. Two months after the release of *Aar Paar*, Geeta and Guru Dutt's first son, Tarun, was born on 9 July 1954. Tarun shared his birthday with Guru Dutt. Geeta, for the time being, got busy with the child. The singing had again taken a backseat. Guru Dutt, meanwhile, had begun to work on his next film.

Geeta admired Guru Dutt's relentless passion for his work. She said in an interview, 'From where does the inspiration come which causes those divine fires in the creator, fires which result in his frenzied seeking after artistic perfection? Where indeed? This question often strikes me when I watch my husband at work. I never cease to wonder at the devotion with which he works, his passion for perfection, the zeal which makes him forget people, circumstances, and the mundane, everyday realities. And I asked myself: "What is the secret of this frenzy? From where does it come?"'[66]

With new found success and money, Guru and Geeta's lifestyle too had undergone a change. From their moderate house, the family shifted to a five-room apartment called Seth Nivas on 16th Road, Khar. Those days, actress Smriti Biswas was close to Guru and Geeta. She remembered, 'We lived in Khar and met every day. Often I'd have dinner with them. Guru liked Konkani food. Geeta's tiffin came from her mother's house. She enjoyed macher jhol and other fish delicacies...Narang saab [Smriti's husband] was a member of the boating club in Powai. We had a floating shack there where all of us went fishing.'

Guru Dutt also bought some farm land in Lonavla (near Poona) to do farming. He built a cosy two-room flat there with all facilities for comfortable living. During this period of time the Lonavla farmhouse was witness to many excursions and good times. Abrar Alvi and Johnny Walker were regular visitors. 'We were all friends. We'd travel together for shikar [hunting], for holidays. Our professional ties also brought us together. We were both part of Guru Dutt's troupe,' said Abrar Alvi. Those were the good times.

This was also the time when friends and family members witnessed a peculiar dichotomy in Guru Dutt's personality. He aspired to be a successful filmmaker and wanted to make great films but he hated being a part of the glamour of the film industry. He was totally missing from the party circuit and gave very few interviews to the film magazines. *Filmfare* magazine describing Guru Dutt's personality in a cover story as, 'Never impolite, Guru could chill a tentative move to friendship with monosyllabic responses or absent-minded nods. Exchange of words to him apparently is no light matter—they are an act of commitment...when warming up to any subject, he talks in a soft, low voice, looking at the world through spectacled eyes, introspective and mildly quizzical, smoking almost continuously and occasionally helping himself to a chew out of a little silver paan-dan. He can joke at himself (I was bad at mathematics; I still am).'[67]

Strangely, after *Aar Paar* clicked, his introvert nature had started taking over. He'd started loving solitude more. The Lonavla farmhouse became his regular escape. 'He loved a quiet life...whenever he felt depressed or had time on his hands, he used to go there and spend a few days. Sometimes he went there with his scripwriter. A couple was engaged to look after the farm. He would ask them to prepare Bajra roti and hot chutney which he loved. Sometimes he himself would cook khichdi,' wrote his mother Vasanthi.

Dev Anand, too, noticed, 'He suffered from melancholia. He was a good man, a good thinker, but a back-bencher. He never wanted to be part of a crowd. He was shy, but good at his work.'[68] Guru's brother, Atmaram, recalled in an interview that he would get irritated with parties or family functions. He worked round the clock and sometimes he would go straight from the studio to his farm house, resulting in arguments and fights with Geeta.

Unlike her husband, Geeta was sociable and felt at home in the glitter of the film world. She wasn't able to devote much time to her career due to her responsibilities as a mother. It frustrated the artist in her. To take her mind off the disappointment, she spent a lot of time with her friends. She organised regular get-togethers at her house and wanted Guru Dutt to participate. Guru Dutt hated it. To him, the peace at the Lonavla farmhouse seemed like heaven. Vasanthi wrote, 'Geeta was fond of glamour and publicity. She hardly liked staying at Lonavla. They always differed in their tastes and opinions, but sometimes they patched up their disagreements.'[69]

Interestingly, Guru Dutt's next film was a take on the modern marriage. The plot of the film was about a supposed sham marriage, for financial benefit, turning into a real one. The lead character was of a 'modern girl' who undergoes a change of heart after observing a traditional Indian housewife.

It was called *Mr. & Mrs. '55*.

31

MR. & MRS. '55

> 'It was an unsaid rule that no one, not even close friends or family members were welcomed when Guru Dutt was immersed in shooting. He wanted no distractions or disturbances on his sets.'
>
> —V.K. Murthy

With *Mr. & Mrs. '55*, Guru Dutt and Abrar Alvi once again proved their mettle in a romantic comedy with great sophistication. Guru Dutt repeated almost the same winning team of *Aar Paar* with Abrar Alvi, V.K. Murthy, the O.P. Nayyar-Geeta Dutt-Mohd Rafi combination and lyrics by Majrooh Sultanpuri. Commercially, the results were even better than *Aar Paar.* The big star, Madhubala, led the cast and lifted the film with her screen presence, her talent for comedy and her spontaneity. However, in this film too the first choice for the male lead role wasn't Guru Dutt but Sunil Dutt. Guru Dutt later felt he would do the role himself.

Praising Guru Dutt's direction and acting performance, the *Filmfare* magazine (27 May 1955) review said:

> Under Guru Dutt's sure handed direction the entire cast embellish the picture with high histrionic appeal, their portrayals breathing life into the story and investing the characterisations with utterly convincing human attributes. Guru Dutt, as the impecunious hero who gambles for love, interprets his role perfectly and displays the genius of the born actor.

Filmfare also praised Johnny Walker's performance, calling it his finest performance to date and one of the year's best. O.P. Nayyar composed ten evergreen tracks out of which, Geeta's voice was present in seven. As a composer, Nayyar was vital to Guru Dutt films in the years during which Guru was evolving into a brilliant filmmaker. His collaboration with O.P. Nayyar was a constant in his formative films. Today we might dismiss these earlier films of Guru Dutt when compared to his celebrated trilogy (*Pyaasa*, *Kaagaz Ke Phool* and *Sahib Biwi aur Ghulam*), but these are the unconventional films with sparkling music by Nayyar that became Guru Dutt's first steps towards his best works.

Guru Dutt planned his song situations as seriously as his dramatic scenes. He was of the view that it was the way a song is presented that drew a repeat audience to the theatres.[70] Guru Dutt's vision and V.K. Murthy's remarkable close-ups, smooth camera movements, signature tracking shots and the play of light and shade gave the film and the songs a distinct feel and texture. Guru Dutt shot 'Jaane kahan mera jigar gaya ji' with the camera moving fluidly under office desks, 'Chal diye banda navaz' was picturised among women drying out saris. In the climactic qawwali 'Karavan dil ka loota', Guru and Murthy go back to their favourite light and shadow play with the half-lit face of the hero to convey the emotional turbulence. The lively 'Thandi hawa kaali ghata' was shot at the Mahatma Gandhi swimming pool in Bombay's Shivaji Park. During the shooting of the song, the director was initially indesicive about the camera angles and movements so the shooting was taking a long time. In such situations, Guru Dutt used to get impateint and very irritated. 'On sets he would shout and get bad-tempered when things did not go right. But it was part of his spirit and I didn't feel bad. I shouted back at him too. In charge of the camera and the lights, I made the heroines look good and so I was very popular among them, and he would mockingly sulk and say, "Main director hoon, mujhse baat nahin karti!"'[71] V.K. Murthy recalled.[72]

It was an unsaid rule that no one, not even close friends or family members were welcomed when Guru Dutt was immersed in shooting. He wanted no distractions or disturbances on his sets.

Looking back, it seems Guru Dutt's self-obsession with his lead characters focused on how society owed them something. Iqbal Masud, distinguished film critic and writer, makes this sharp observation: 'It is the fashion today, to regard *Aar Paar* (1954) and *Mr. & Mrs. '55* (1955) as slick and successful commercials. So they were. But if you look at the pattern of those films carefully, you will notice remarkable similarities in the big three—*Pyaasa*, *Kagaz Ke Phool*, and *Saheb Bibi Aur Ghulam*. We have the young dissentients (taxi driver and cartoonist in the two films) at odds with society, willing to make a fast buck but unwilling to sell themselves, and remaining loyal to a true love. It is the same romanticism, the same defiant search for some beauty, pure, innocent, untamed that marks the greater films. Only later the search grows more desperate, the costs of failure rise higher, death starts to wait in the wings to confer welcome release.'

Mr. & Mrs. '55 carries a strong influence of Hollywood romantic comedies. The characters as well as the situations are treated with breezy humour and satire. But post this film, Guru Dutt's cinematic characters became serious and the tone of the films got dark and darker.

Section Eight

DESTRUCTION OF A DREAM

1955–59: BOMBAY

'Johnny, I don't think I know how to direct films.'

32

INDECISIVE, UNSURE GENIUS

'The moment he felt that the film was not shaping up well, he lost inspiration. No amount of advice, or fear of monetary loss could make him carry on the project.'

—Abrar Alvi

As a director at the helm after *Mr. & Mrs. '55*, Guru Dutt went on to make his masterpiece *Pyaasa* and then after the *Gouri* fiasco came the quasi-autobiographical *Kaagaz Ke Phool.* India's first cinemascope film—made using the anamorphic lenses brought in from Hollywood originally for the film *Gouri* which ended up to be this film.

As a film producer Guru Dutt had earlier decided on a rule that he would make a commercial entertainer for every serious 'artistic' film that he made. But despite being a serious subject, *Pyaasa* was an unexpected success. It elated him so much that he thought another similar theme would also be accepted by the audience. So, skipping his usual policy of making a commercial entertainer in between, he selected a serious subject again.

While *Pyaasa* was based on the feelings and experiences from his early years of struggle, *Kaagaz Ke Phool* emerged from his impressions about life as a filmmaker dealing with problems in his personal life, ultimately leading to neglect and indifference towards his work. The filmmaker was played by Guru Dutt, his muse was Waheeda Rahman.

Those were the days when publicity booklets were printed to announce the new films. The publicity booklet of *Kaagaz Ke Phool* contained the announcement about two more films from Guru Dutt films: *Raaz* and *Chaudavin Ka Chand* with a caption that read:

'Two more box office smashers in the Guru Dutt tradition'

During the planning of *Kaagaz Ke Phool,* Guru Dutt's trusted asistant director and A-team member Raj Khosla had already left the company. Another assistant Niranjan, who had assisted Guru in his previous four films, was roped in to direct the suspense thriller *Raaz.* The story of *Raaz* was based on the novel *The Woman in White* by Wilkie Collins. Waheeda Rehman was cast in a double role of two sisters while actor Sunil Dutt of *Mother India* fame was signed in the lead role of a military doctor. The poster of *Raaz* only had Waheeda Rehman with a 'fast progressing' tag on the right corner.

The filming of *Raaz* began in the picturesque snow-clad town of Shimla. But soon, Sunil Dutt was out of the film. He was very upset as there was no reason given to him for his ouster. And then soon came the news that Guru Dutt was now to play the lead role instead.

The gossip magazines went into a tizzy. They spun out stories that Guru did not wish for anyone else to play the role of Waheeda's love interest. After a disturbed schedule, the shooting resumed in Shimla and big money was spent on the schedule and set up of a military hospital. Two songs were recorded by composer R.D. Burman, who was making his debut as a music director with the film.

From Shimla, Guru Dutt wrote a letter to his sons Tarun and Arun (four years and one year old, respectively) in which he wrote that he missed his family but work never seems to end. In a very loaded statement, Guru Dutt wrote to his sons, 'When you grow up, I want you to remember that work is the most important thing of all. A person who doesn't work is a fool. So let me finish the work I am doing and then I'll be back.'

Was this message really meant for his kids (four years and one year old)? Or did he intend to convey it to Geeta?

Back in Bombay, when Guru Dutt edited the scenes they had shot in Shimla, he did not like them. So, staying true to his style, Dutt scrapped them and abandoned the film *Raaz* despite spending so much time and money on it.

'Guru Dutt Ji shelved the film. When we asked why, he said, "Nahin jam raha hai" [It isn't working],' said Waheeda Rehman.[73]

Screenwriter Abrar Alvi wrote, 'He was the Hamlet of films. He has often been accused of vacillation and fickle-mindedness; of starting films and dropping them. Having known the man very closely I can say he was a very restless man—but genuine and sincere to the core. If a subject inspired him, on an impulse he would start the film. But as he went along creating, his critical faculties would also have full play. The moment he felt that the film was not shaping up well, he lost inspiration. No amount of advice, or fear of monetary loss could make him carry on the project once the inspiration was gone.'

Dev Anand said, 'He always looked and felt melancholic. He had a great cinematic sense and rhythm but would shoot and shoot and shoot, wasting a lot of footage. He was indecisive and unsure. We used to meet regularly even after Baazi but gradually both of us got busier.

'He was always sincere when he started a film—he was equally sincere when he dropped it,' said Abrar Alvi.

33

WAQT KE SITAM

'Don't make this film, it's just your personal life.'

—S.D. Burman to Guru Dutt

The thirty-four-year-old Guru Dutt had lost huge money as two projects, *Gouri* and *Raaz*, were shelved successively after expensive shooting schedules. There was also the pressure of the distributors to make another profitable film soon. Guru Dutt also had a studio to run with a big staff.

On many occasions, Guru Dutt would even pay the artists signed for the shelved films. Abrar Alvi said, 'If with the cancellation of a film in the making, some people who had got a break in that film, found their hopes ending—Guru Dutt's heart bled for them. For days I have seen him sulky and morose, not because his money went down the drain, but because he felt he had let down these people. He did not even have the heart to face them and people misunderstood. If only people could have understood his innate sincerity to his art.'

But this explanation sounds too simplistic and cannot be attributed to just his perfectionism. This is not how film production works across the world. Shelving films at such regular intervals can't be a normal thing. In fact, people close to Guru Dutt knew that his personal life was going through a turbulent phase. Even after a suicide attempt, he was subjected to more turmoil, heartbreak and professional pressures to deliver—something that did not come naturally to the artistic soul in him.

Sometimes he would just leave the studio and seek far-off places to escape the mayhem of his life. At other times he would go straight to his farmhouse in Lonavala. As a form of escape, he seriously considered farming. He stayed there for a few days and often got friendly with the local people. But he realised that farming required hard work, more time and regular trips—so he soon gave up the idea. Instead, the ever curious Guru Dutt did a strange thing. Advised by the local people, he set up a small brewery in his farmhouse.[74] He took his close friends to flaunt it and taste the beer produced by his fully operational brewery. But everyone knew that it was Guru Dutt's escape mechanism at work. Once the curiosity was satisfied, the brewery was uprooted and he had to go back to the life he wanted to escape from.

The professional and personal stress was incessantly playing on his mind while he was making his most expensive and ambitious film *Kaagaz Ke Phool.*

The brooding, quasi-autobiographical *Kaagaz Ke Phool* mirrors Guru Dutt's own story, his now unhappy marriage with his wife and his confused relationship with his muse. It also eerily ends with the death of the filmmaker after failing to come to terms with his acute loneliness and doomed relationships.

Guru Dutt's brother Devi Dutt recalled,[75] 'Guru Dutt had an ego and that caused problems.' Even while he was making the film *Kaagaz Ke Phool*, music director S.D. Burman had warned him to not attempt it.

S.D. Burman told him, 'Don't make this film, it's just your personal life.'

Guru Dutt shot back, 'You concentrate on your music. Let me do my work.'

The two never worked together after that.

Guru Dutt gave his heart and soul to this intensely personal film, as if to paint his real pain on-screen to release and heal from it. Shot in CinemaScope, *Kaagaz Ke Phool* had glaring flaws—a patchy script and inconsistent characters—but visually the imagery, the light and shadow play Dutt and Murthy achieved was sheer magic on celluloid. Some sequences remain with you long after you have watched the film.

Unfolding in a flashback, *Kaagaz Ke Phool* is the story of a successful filmmaker Suresh Sinha (Guru Dutt). Sinha is separated from his wife and has a teenage daughter. He meets Shanti (Waheeda Rehman) and grooms her as an actress. Shanti becomes a famous star and the two develop a close emotional bond. But their relationship becomes the fodder for gossip columns. Unable to take the taunts of her friends in school, Sinha's daughter requests Shanti to go away from Sinha's life. The relationship is doomed. After Shanti leaves, Suresh is also denied access to his daughter by the court. A devastated Sinha finds solace in alcohol. His films fail and his career goes downhill. He loses everything, and in the end, dies a lonely and forgotten man, sitting in the director's chair, in the same film studio where he once reigned.

In *Pyaasa,* the lead character of the poet had renounced the world and had left for a better place. In *Kaagaz Ke Phool,* Guru Dutt takes the same theme forward but here the renunciation is not symbolic. He chooses death over a society where no one cares for an artist or his desolation.

The song, 'Waqt ne kiya kya haseen sitam' is still talked about as one of the best picturisations ever and a grand tribute to the studio system of the 1940s of Indian cinema. The idea of two lead protagonists voicing their emotions without moving their lips looked ethereal. The light beam effect created using huge mirrors and natural sunlight was spectacular and is still rated among one of the best photographed songs of all time.

Cinematographer V.K. Murthy and art director M.R. Achrekar got Filmfare Awards for their seminal work. Murthy shared an anecdote, 'The *Kaagaz Ke Phool* premier was held in Bombay. The film fraternity was there. During the interval, Shammi Kapoor asked loudly, "Where is the hero of the film?" Someone pointed to Guru Dutt but Shammi Kapoor hoisted me up and went around the lobby, screaming, "Here is the hero of the film."'[76]

It was in 2010, fifty-one years after filming *Kaagaz Ke Phool*, that V.K. Murthy was honoured with the Dadasaheb Phalke Award. He was eighty-six then and still remains the only 'technical' talent to win a Phalke Award—the highest award in cinema in India.

Over the years the film has developed a cult following and it's been taught at many film schools across the world. But when it released in 1959, *Kaagaz ke Phool* was an instant disaster at the box office. Almost all the reviews tore it apart. *Filmindia* (November 1959) though praised it for its technical achievements but wrote it off saying, '*Kaagaz Ke Phool* is an utterly undistinguished picture except that it is made in CinemaScope. It is a depressing, incoherent tale boringly told.'

Guru Dutt's cousin and renowned filmmaker Shyam Benegal adds, 'What I remember most of all is the preview screening of *Kaagaz Ke Phool*, India's first CinemaScope film. Bimal Roy and other leading lights of the film industry were present. At the end of the screening, there was pin-drop silence. No one said a word. Guru Dutt was absolutely crestfallen.'

V.K. Murthy who worked as hard as Guru Dutt on the film said, 'I had told him after seeing the first eight reels that the film was beautiful, like a poetry, but if the film continues like this, you will not get even a rupee. Why would people watch the biography of a director? They wouldn't even believe that the director was a failure and didn't have money…people are used to seeing tragic ladies, not men. That's why the film failed, I think.'[77]

Expecting a *Pyaasa* kind of reception, Guru Dutt was utterly shocked at the complete rejection of *Kaagaz Ke Phool.* During its premiere at the famous Maratha Mandir theatre in Mumbai, the audience had booed. Raj Khosla found Guru Dutt sitting quietly in a corner in the theatre. He looked at Raj and said, 'Raj, it's a stillborn child…'[78]

'He felt as if the world has suffocated him. He was never the same after that. The financial failure didn't bother him, he didn't care two hoots for money…he was hurt because people didn't understand his film. I remember him telling me, "Raj, I might not have been able to communicate. Kuchh to baat hui hogi".'[79]

Lalitha Lajmi remembers, 'There were even reports of audiences booing as soon as he appears on-screen in the film. He was devastated.'[80]

The grand premiere in Delhi was no different. Guru Dutt had called up his friend, Dev Anand, after the premiere at the iconic Regal theatre in Delhi, 'Dev! My film has been a disaster. Completely rejected.'

'The day he realised that his *Kaagaz Ke Phool* did not do well—he'd gone to Delhi to open it in the presence of President S. Radhakrishnan—he was a sad man. He never went behind the camera to direct; he only acted. He took Abrar [Alvi], but never had the courage to direct. Woh cheez khatam ho gayi thhi,'[81] Dev Anand later said.[82]

In an interview with author Nasreen Munni Kabir,[83] poet-lyricist Kaifi Azmi remembers, 'Bahut kareeb ho gaye the jab humne saath kaam kiya tha. Main samajhta hoon yahi gana, "Bichhde sabhi baari baari..." yahi kahaani thi unki jo shayad screen pe woh us dhang se nahi kah paaye.'[84]

Remembering the debacle of *Kaagaz Ke Phool*, Johhny Walker would say, '*Kaagaz Ke Phool* ke premier mein public ne humko joote-chappal markar nikala. Public said, "What a disastrous film you've made!" Guru Dutt came out of the theatre and said, "I can't direct anymore." And he never did. Because he lost his confidence after that.'

Drowning in self-pity, Guru Dutt told Johnny Walker, 'Johnny, I don't think I know how to direct films. I have lost it yaar.'[85]

And after that Guru Dutt went into a shell.

34

HUM RAHE NA HUM

> 'In the formula-ridden film world of ours, one who ventures to go out of the beaten track is condemned to the definition which Mathew Arnold used for Shelley…"An angel beating his wings in a void."'
>
> —Guru Dutt

As an actor Guru Dutt never looked and acted better before or since *Kaagaz Ke Phool.* His eyes exuding pain, the turmoil and confusion in his character's life and career blurred the line between fiction and reality. The film media and gossip columns were unanimous in calling it 'the story of Guru Dutt's life'. Many scenes were also compared to the situations in the personal life of Guru Dutt.

There's a peculiar scene of a film within the film. In *Kaagaz Ke Phool*, the filmmaker Suresh Sinha is making a film—*Devdas*.[86] The actress playing the lead female character is obsessing over having a fancy hairstyle and a flambouyant dress for the shooting schedule. She wants to look glamorous. However, her director Suresh Sinha wants her to look simple and rustic according to the background of her character. An argument ensues and finally Suresh Sinha puts his foot down on her demands.

A situation very similar to what had happened on the sets of *Gouri*.

Kaagaz Ke Phool surprisingly did not have the credits for its story.

Whose story was *Kaagaz Ke Phool*? While it is often said to be inspired from the 1954 Hollywood classic *A Star is Born*, there was a lesser known controversy on the writing credits of *Kaagaz Ke Phool*. The screenwriter Nabendu Ghosh who had worked with Guru Dutt in *Aar Paar*, *Gouri* (shelved) and *Raaz* (shelved) had penned a story about a writer and his muse. Guru Dutt loved the story and asked Ghosh to write the screenplay.

At that point in time the author was busy scripting Bimal Roy's classic *Devdas*. He could not meet the director. Apparently, Guru Dutt took offence and engaged another screenwriter, borrowing the basic storyline from Nabendu Ghosh's story. Nabendu Ghosh's daughter, the journalist and author Ratnottama Sengupta says, 'Guru Dutt also made certain changes in the story and turned it into that of a film-maker and his muse.' What's notable is when *Kaagaz Ke Phool* film released in 1959, the story was not attributed to anybody, only the screenplay was attributed to the new screenwriter. So an upset Nabendu Ghosh met Guru Dutt and asked, 'This is my story, why isn't my name there in the credit titles?' The director replied, 'I have changed it—I have personalized it, now it is my story.'

The legendary screenwriter went on record about this controversy in his autobiography *Eka Naukar Jatri* where he concludes the entire story, saying, 'I was deprived of being the writer of *Kaagaz Ke Phool* forever.'

There's no version of Guru Dutt on this issue.

In *Kaagaz Ke Phool,* the relationship between the director and his muse (played by Waheeda Rehman) is conveyed only through intense expresssions, gestures and uncommunicated feelings. Throughout the film their relationship remains symbolic with no real romantic scenes. Their feelings communicated through the unsaid words and gestures are both poetic and beautiful. But the depiction of this platonic relationship where everything remains unsaid confused the audiences. Kaifi Azmi clearly remembered Dutt's confusion and how he struggled to communicate his feelings during the making of the film, 'Guru Dutt was a great craftsman behind the camera. Lekin jo baatein camera ke through khhobsurati se samjha dete the, woh is tarah express karne mein bahot kamzor the. Woh khud kya chahte hain ye batane mein unko bahot mushkil hoti thi. Unki yeh kamzori thi ki woh apne ko express nahi kar paate the.'[87]

Many associates and close friends have said on record that even while the film was being shot, his state of mind was far from balanced. The situation at home was volatile leading to major mood swings and his indecisiveness was also at its peak. He had also majorly overshot the film, shooting long sequences and scrapping them after he was unsure, wasting much money and resources. Kaifi Azmi recalled, 'Jab release hui to kisi ki samajh mein nahi aaya ki kahna kya chah rahe hain. Aur us waqt unki mental haalat bhi aisi thi ki woh clear nahi the. Domestic life bhi unki bahot uljhi hui thi. To kahani change hoti chali gayi. Ye jitni film release hui hain issey zyada wahan kat ke dabbon mei padi hogi.'[88]

Lalitha Lajmi said that Guru Dutt took the failure to heart and never recovered from it as long as he was alive. Guru Dutt himself said in an interview later that the film 'went over the heads' of the audience.

In an essay titled 'Classics and Cash', Guru Dutt wrote, 'In the formula-ridden film world of ours, one who ventures to go out of the beaten track is condemned to the definition which Mathew Arnold used for Shelley…"An angel beating his wings in a void."'

Waheeda Rehman recalled, 'He used to say, "Life mein, yaar, kya hai? Do hi toh cheezen hai—kamyaabi aur failure. There is nothing in between.'[89]

After the dismal failure of *Kaagaz Ke Phool,* Guru Dutt never officially directed a film again.

35

ONE FOR ALL, ALL FOR ONE

> 'Enough of self-pity! *Hum sab banaate hain na film saath mein, milkar*!'
>
> —Johnny Walker

The failure of *Kaagaz Ke Phool* caused a major financial disruption in Dutt's life. He couldn't pay salaries to his staff for two months and asked some of his senior people, including writer Abrar Alvi, to look for work outside his film company. Guru badly needed a successful film to keep his company solvent. It was also decided that he will take up acting roles in other productions.

It was Abrar Alvi, Johnny Walker and Rehman who told him, 'Enough of self-pity. We know you're sad but you can't sit forever and do nothing. You have to start working on a new film.' Guru Dutt replied, 'But I don't know how to make films, so how do I make one?'

Johnny Walker knew Guru Dutt already had a script for a social drama ready. Having earlier worked with director M. Sadiq, popularly know as Sadiq Babu in the industry,

Johnny said, 'You don't worry, I'll get Sadiq Babu to direct. You just act in the film and produce it.' So together 'Team Guru Dutt' forced him to begin the film *Chaudhvin Ka Chand*.

Nasir, Johnny Walker's son, remembers, 'If you know how the film industry functions, you will know that if a big film flops, the stars are usually averse to working with the film-maker. But their bond was so strong. Everyone said, "Theek hai yaar, hum sab banaate hain na film saath mein, milkar!"[90] It wasn't just filmmaking for them, it was about standing with Guru Dutt.' It was one for all, all for one.

Guru Dutt had to plan more films and agreed to complete his next, *Chaudavin Ka Chand*, in a few months to keep the studio running. Despite the storm going on in his life, Guru Dutt, with the support of his team, took up the challenge and decided to fight back.

But even in these desperate times, Guru Dutt didn't stop dreaming. He wished to make a film in colour. So he sent his trusted cinematographer Murthy to London to learn about the technicalities of colour photography. Murthy was asked to observe a unit of Carl Foreman's war film *The Guns of Navarone*. With Murthy gone, Abrar Alvi also signed a few films of other producers as asked by Guru Dutt. This meant Guru Dutt had to make *Chaudhvin Ka Chand* without two key members of his team.

The casting, however, included the Guru Dutt regulars. He and Waheeda Rehman were going to play the lead romantic roles, while other crucial roles went to Rehman and Johnny Walker.

Chaudhvin Ka Chand was based on an original story 'Ek Jhalak' (A Glimpse) by writer Shaukat Hussain Rizvi. It was a love story set in the North Indian city of Lucknow. It belongs to the popular genre then known as 'Muslim social', which used to be a successful genre in Hindi cinema for many decades. Guru Dutt also felt that Sadiq, being from an Urdu-speaking Muslim background, would be the apt person to convey the culture, etiquettes and customs of the Muslim society.

Guru Dutt wanted the top music director, Naushad, to compose music for *Chaudhvin Ka Chand*. But due to the financial crunch, he realised he couldn't afford Naushad. So he opted for music director Ravi Shankar Sharma, popularly known as Ravi.

Remembering *Chaudhvin Ka Chand*, Ravi said in an interview, 'I was in the process of establishing myself while Guru Dutt was a well-known and revered name by then. When I was called by him before the commencement of the work for *Chaudhvin Ka Chand*, the message worried and even upset me. People began to warn me that he was quite a difficult taskmaster and I too had my doubts. But it was a total contrast when I met him. He was so simple and straightforward.'[91]

The team of *Chaudhvin Ka Chand* was complete. Though the subject of the film wasn't close to Guru Dutt's sensibilities as a film-maker, he was in need of a commercial success.

It was also clear that despite the heartbreak of *Kaagaz Ke Phool*, he was still dreaming of making a classic. As *Chaudhvin Ka Chand* went on floors, Guru Dutt was already thinking about his next 'artistic' film.

36

BIMAL MITRA

'It was just a three-minute conversation. But there was something special in his voice.'

—Bimal Mitra

It was early morning in Calcutta when the doorbell rang at writer Bimal Mitra's house. The gentleman at the door introduced himself as Surya Ladia, the Calcutta distributor of Guru Dutt Films. Bursting with excitement he told Bimal Mitra that Guru Dutt wants to make a film on Mitra's novel *Saheb Bibi Golam*.

Ladia said that Guru Dutt had sent an air ticket and would wish to meet him in Bombay. Before Mitra could speak, the overexcited distributor added that Mitra would be staying at Guru Dutt's palatial bungalow in Bombay and since Guru Dutt's wife is a Bengali, Mitra would be treated with authentic Bengali food.

Bimal Mitra was amused at this conversation but he kept listening quietly till the excited Surya Ladia paused. Then Bimal Mitra replied that he was busy writing his new novel, so it would not be possible for him to go to Bombay. Surya Ladia was shocked. He came to meet Mitra thinking that he would jump with joy at the offer. But Mitra was adamant that he cannot go. So finally Ladia requested and convinced Mitra to come to his office in the evening for a phone (trunk) call with Guru Dutt. Bimal Mitra agreed.

'If you don't want to give me the rights of your novel, I would not force you. But please come and be my guest,' said Guru Dutt in his honeyed voice over a phone call that evening. Bimal Mitra recalled, 'It was just a three-minute conversation. But there was something special in his voice.'

The next day at 3.30 PM Bimal Mitra's flight landed at the Santacruz Airport, Bombay.

From the airport, the car took him to Guru Dutt's Pali Hill bungalow. Bimal Mitra was amazed looking at the expansive bungalow. He saw some people were standing to receive him in the portico. As the car stopped, Guru Dutt said 'Namaskar'. Wearing a kurta and a silk lungi and chewing pan, Guru Dutt introduced himself to Bimal Mitra. He was talking in chaste Bangla that impressed Bimal Mitra, 'Before I had met Guru Dutt, I had not imagined that a person's smile can be so beautiful. I had never seen his movies but I was totally moved by seeing his smile.'

'This is my wife, Geeta Dutt,' said Guru while Geeta greeted Mitra with a namaste.

Inside the bungalow there were animal skins (bear skin, leopard skin) displayed to their full natural glory on the walls. The conversation began casually about the film industry and films. Then it veered towards his novel, *Saheb*

Bibi Golam, when Geeta entered the room and asked Mitra, 'What would you like to have for dinner, Bimal Da?'

'Please make something light and bland for me. I can't have spicy food.'

Guru who was having tea asked, 'Tell me, who should be cast for the character of Jaba? Do you have someone in mind?'

'I don't know much about the artists here…' replied Bimal Mitra.

Guru said, 'I was thinking, I should give that role to Waheeda.'

'Who is she?' asked Mitra.

'One of my artists—Waheeda Rehman. Very impressive and proficient actress.'

'I realised Geeta Dutt's face turned serious,' wrote Bimal Mitra.

At that time, Bimal Mitra did not have a clue that more than being a part of an iconic Guru Dutt film *Sahib Bibi Aur Ghulam* (1962), he was going to closely witness the disintegration of their lives.

37

MAN OF IDEAS

> 'If I had thought about benefit [profit] and loss, I would have been some other kind of person. For me, my ideas are more important than any profit or loss.'
>
> —Guru Dutt

Guru Dutt took Bimal Mitra to his studio where a song sequence of *Chaudhvin Ka Chand* was being shot. It was the first time Mitra had seen a film shooting. He got bored after Guru Dutt took the twelfth 'take' of a shot. The sequence finally got okayed after three long hours.

Later, the conversation again turned towards *Saheb Bibi Golam*. Guru Dutt said, 'Bimal Babu, everyone is discouraging me from making this film. Even my wife is stopping me. But come what may, I am going to make this film. Actually I am a very stubborn person. If I decide something, I don't listen to anybody.'

'But such behaviour harms you a lot,' said Bimal Mitra.

'Yes, but I don't care.'

'It is better to seek the opinion of others. It can only benefit.'

Guru Dutt replied, 'If I had thought about benefit [profit] and loss, I would have been some other kind of person. For me, my ideas are more important than any profit or loss. That's why I have a request.'

'What request?'

Guru Dutt requested Bimal Mitra to write the script of the film based on his novel. Bimal Mitra agreed. Guru Dutt suggested that Mitra could shift to the Lonavala farmhouse the very next day to write in peace.

But before that Geeta wanted to speak with Bimal Mitra.

After breakfast the next morning when Guru Dutt went to his room to get ready, Geeta Dutt asked Bimal Mitra, 'Ok, so do you know finally who has been cast for the role of Jaba?'

'Yes, that girl Waheeda Rehman.'

'Why? Is there no other actress in the Bombay film industry?' asked Geeta Dutt.

'Why do you say so? That girl seems nice. Guru Dutt introduced me to her. He had great faith in her talent. Guru was telling me…'

'Do you know, because of the same Waheeda Rehman, there is so much disturbance in my family life/household,' said Geeta.

Section Nine

BUILDING OF A DREAM

1955–56

'Guru Ji was a different man;
another like him I haven't met again.'

38

WAHEEDA COMES TO BOMBAY

'They are they and I am me.'

—Waheeda Rehman

Towards the end of 1955, Waheeda Rehman landed in Bombay with her mother. She had been summoned by Guru Dutt for his next production after the success of *Mr. & Mrs. '55*.

After directing a not-so-successful independent film, *Milap*, Raj Khosla came back to assist Guru Dutt who asked him to direct his next production—the crime thriller *C.I.D.* starring Dev Anand and Shakila. *C.I.D.* is now known for another crucial milestone for Guru Dutt films. The debut of Waheeda Rehman.

While discussing names from the Bombay film industry for a supporting female role, Guru Dutt remembered the girl he had met few months ago in Hyderabad while on a road trip there to meet his South India distributor. He thought of casting Waheeda Rehman in the role. Though there was some resistance within the team about the casting—for such roles normally went to glamorous actresses while Waheeda had traditional, plain looks. But Guru Dutt had made up his mind. The film distributor, Manubhai, who used to handle the distribution of Mysore and Hyderabad territories for Guru Dutt films, was asked to get in touch with Waheeda.

Waheeda recalled, 'One afternoon a fat man who called himself Manubhai Patel wanted to meet me at my residence. He said Mr Guru Dutt would like to see me and I should go to Bombay.'

When Waheeda Rehman landed in Bombay with her mother, they were taken to the Ritz Hotel in Churchgate and told that Guru Dutt would meet them the next day in the studio for talks and the signing of the contract. It was surely a golden chance for a young girl from the south of India to work in a Guru Dutt film opposite the big star Dev Anand. Any actress would be more than excited to sign on the dotted line. But Waheeda Rehman was different.

What followed in the meeting the following day surprised Guru Dutt and his team. This was something a young girl getting her golden chance in the film world never does.

It was the Famous Studios in Mahalaxmi where Guru Dutt had an office on the first floor. Guru Dutt, Raj Khosla, Abrar Alvi, V.K. Murthy, Guruswamy and assistant director

Niranjan were waiting there for Waheeda. 'He [Guru Dutt] was quietly sitting and watching me while most of the talking was done by director Raj Khosla, production controller Guruswamy and writer Abrar Alvi,' Waheeda remembered. They were ready with a contract that had to be signed by Waheeda's mother as Waheeda was still a minor (not yet eighteen years of age).

Before anything could be decided, Raj Khosla said that her name is too long and it had to be changed. This startled Waheeda 'I asked them why. So they said that everyone does it, Madhubala's name wasn't Madhubala. Nargis' name isn't Nargis. So I said, "They are they and I am me."'[92]

The meeting had started on a wrong note. Guru Dutt tried to convince Waheeda to change her name but she was adamant. Raj Khosla got irritated. 'So they told my mother: "Mrs Rehman, do one thing. Take your daughter back and make her study further and make her a lawyer. Because the way she argues—not like this, not like that." Raj Khosla said, "Guru, just think about what you are getting into,"' recalled Waheeda.

Guru Dutt as usual was silently sitting with his hand under his chin and his elbow resting on the table, observing everything with a smirk on his face. He politely told Waheeda and her mother that he needed time to think. The contract signing was postponed for a few days.

Waheeda was unfazed. As a young girl in a new city surrounded by seniors who looked shocked at her behaviour, she displayed enormous grit and a will to live a life on her terms.

Her demeanour had made Raj Khosla very angry. But perhaps Guru Dutt was impressed.

Their next meeting was to be even more dramatic.

39

KAHIN PE NIGAHEIN, KAHIN PE NISHANA

'He was a different man; another like him I haven't met again.'

—Waheeda on Guru

Guru Dutt agreed to her demand of going ahead with her real name. The contract was ready. For the first year she was to be paid Rs 1200/- per month. Waheeda's mother was asked to sign the contract. But before she could sign, Waheeda interrupted again saying she would like to add something to the contract. Raj Khosla was astonished.

A surprised Guru Dutt asked, 'Are you not happy?'[93]

'I will be happy when I am satisfied with my costumes,' said Waheeda

'Don't worry, all the costumes will be to your satisfaction and you won't be forced to put on the dress which you don't like…is that alright?' asked Guru Dutt.

'It will be alright, if this is mentioned in the contract,' replied Waheeda.

'Don't you believe me?' he asked.

'Well, it is not that. But don't you think it would be better if you put this in the agreement?'

Raj Khosla was stunned at the demands of the new girl. He had begun wondering if she was going to create problems on his sets.

But Guru Dutt relented. The clause about the costumes was added to the contract. Finally her mother Mumtaz Begum signed the contract. Waheeda smiled. This was the beginning of a new chapter in Guru Dutt's filmography.

Meanwhile, the shooting of *C.I.D.* had begun and was already on full steam. Waheeda had shifted to Bombay and was given a flat near Guru Dutt's house where she lived with her mother Mumtaz Begum, her elder sister, Sayeeda, and brother-in-law Rauf. People close to Guru Dutt remember that Waheeda and her mother were regular at Guru Dutt's house during get-togethers.

Guru Dutt's younger brother and film producer, Devi Dutt, who was an integral part of Guru Dutt Films Pvt. Ltd., said, 'Waheeda Ji was simple looking; she was not like Meena Kumari or Madhubala. For black and white films, the make-up would be heavy. So her features looked sharp. She was reserved and sober and had an endearing way of saying "aadab".'

They were shooting the song 'Kahin pe nigahen kahin

pe nishana' when director Raj Khosla's fear about Waheeda came true. In the sequence, Waheeda's character had to sing a seductive song and there was a glamorous dress she had to wear but she flatly refused. 'I was too shy. And there was a lace blouse. So I told them that I'm not going to wear the dress. It's too lacy. It has to have some lining, or give me a dupatta. So he [Khosla] said: "No. You are a vamp and you are trying to seduce the villain." So I said: "No, I don't care. I'm not going to wear a dress like that. I won't come to the sets."'

It created a flutter. Dev Anand was waiting, the entire team was ready to can the song. The choreographer, Zohra Sehgal, tried to convince her. The costume designer, Bhanu Athaiya, explained her vision behind the costume and tried to make Waheeda understand her point but Waheeda was adamant.

Remembering the day Waheeda says, 'He [Guru Dutt] was out of Bombay. Writing the script of *Pyaasa*. Raj Khosla said, "Dev Anand is waiting." So I said, "I wait for him every day, let him wait." I put my foot down. I thought that if it didn't work out, I would go back. I wanted to work. I was dying to work. But I had certain limitations.'

Raj Khosla reached out to Guru Dutt over a phone call and told him about the drama unfolding on the sets.

Guru Dutt rushed back from Khandala. 'He came back and asked me and my mother, "What's happening?"

'So I said, "I have that clause written in my contract. I don't like this costume."

'So he said, "But it's not vulgar." It had full sleeves.'

Waheeda told him that she would not wear a lace blouse. She wanted a dupatta to cover it or a lining so that it was not transparent. It would have taken a day to put the lining but Dev Anand had to leave for Switzerland the next day.

An irritated Guru Dutt said, 'God, what kind of a woman is this?'

Finally, they had to oblige and give her a dupatta. Raj Khosla was very unhappy. The unit members were surprised and wondered why Guru Dutt was tolerating this behaviour from a newcomer. They had seen Guru Dutt losing his patience with other actors and senior technicians. But he seemed like an entirely different person when talking to Waheeda.

Remembering those days Waheeda later said, 'Yes I did create quite a few problems for him and perhaps any other producer would have never tolerated it. But he was a different man; another like him I haven't met again.'[94]

40

THE LOSS OF GEETA'S STARDOM

'The artist's first love is his work. It is as simple as that.'

—Geeta Dutt

Geeta and Guru Dutt were expecting their second child. Every new project at Guru Dutt Films used to excite Geeta for the possibilities it would bring for her as a singer. She never tired of listening to Guru Dutt talking passionately about the stories he wanted to create on celluloid. The creation of music in his films. Those were the moments in which she loved her life as 'Mrs Guru Dutt' and felt alive. 'The artist's first love is his work. It is as simple as that, really, when everything boils down to the essentials. It appears to be the final explanation of the mystery of all artistic and creative endeavours, be it painting, writing, film-making, dancing or singing,' said Geeta.

Geeta was regularly singing with music composers like O.P. Nayyar, Sardul Kwatra, Chitragupt, Hemant Kumar, N. Dutta, Anil Biswas, etc. but top composers like Naushad, S.D. Burman, Shankar-Jaikishan were generally not approaching her. She was ousted by reigning playback singer Lata Mangeshkar who had become the first choice for every big film-maker and leading composer. She had also realised that one popular album of a Guru Dutt film every year was not enough to secure her a place in the list of top singers. In 1955–56, except the very successful songs of *Mr. & Mrs. '55*, Geeta Dutt sang in B-Grade films like *Society*, *Son of Ali Baba*, *Teen Bhai*, *Tees Maar Khan*, *Aawara Shahzadi*, *Arab Ka Saudagar* and a few more. But no one really remember these films or her songs in them. Yet, whenever she got a chance with a music director of calibre who came with a tripping tune, Geeta Dutt always delivered.

The music of the 1956 film *Bhai Bhai* was composed by the ace composer Madan Mohan. The album was dominated by Madan Mohan's favourite singer, Lata Mangeshkar, who gave her vocals for eight songs in the film (out of eleven). Geeta Dutt just had one song: 'Ae dil mujhe bata de tu kis pe aa gaya hai', which became a humongous hit. Picturised on Shyama, this happy song conveys the innocence and feelings of the first flush of love. The album is still remembered for Geeta's lone chart-buster. Music critic Raju Bharatan had remarked, 'The first thing that strikes one when you hear Geeta Dutt sing was that she never sang. She just glided through a tune. Of all her contemporaries her musical training was perhaps the sketchiest but what she lacked in training and technique, she more than made up with her ability to breathe life and emotion into any song she was singing.'

Madan Mohan composed about ten songs for Geeta between 1955 and 1957, in films like *Pocket Maar* (1956), *Fifty Fifty* (1956) and *Samundar* (1957). Though none could match the success of 'Ae dil mujhe bata de tu kis pe aa gaya hai'. It was also obvious that Geeta was never Madan Mohan's first choice as the lead female singer. Lata Mangeshkar had taken an unprecedented lead as far as voice, technique, discipline and stardom was concerned. She was followed by the then struggling Asha Bhosle who was now getting the kind of songs Geeta specialised in. In fact, music directors like O.P. Nayyar and S.D. Burman who had successfully worked with Geeta Dutt were drifting towards Asha Bhosle.

It was clear that focus on her family life, her marital problems and her inaccessibility for song rehearsals and recordings had affected her career greatly.

Geeta had lost her stardom. While this constantly bothered Geeta, Guru took it as a natural sacrifice for a happy family life.

Section Ten

DESTRUCTION OF A DREAM

1960–61

'I think I'll go mad.'

41

TWO TORMENTED SOULS

> 'The film magazines, film newspapers are the same. People used to propagate such spicy stories about Guru Dutt and an actress that I was ashamed to read them. I felt like committing suicide.'
>
> —Geeta Dutt

The disastrous result of *Kaagaz Ke Phool* at the box-office changed everything in Guru Dutt's professional and personal life.

Till *Kaagaz Ke Phool*, in the films produced by Guru Dutt Films Pvt. Ltd, the female playback voice had been predominantly Geeta Dutt. Geeta's booming voice was instrumental in the success of Guru Dutt's films. Diving neck deep into producing *Chaudhvin Ka Chand*, without talking about the financial and emotional turmoil that he was going through, Guru Dutt drowned himself in the story sittings, song recordings, shoot planning and, of course, alcohol.

With *Chaudhvin Ka Chand,* as most of the A-team

of Guru Dutt moved on, the norm for the lead female playback singer changed too. The predominant female voice used was that of Asha Bhosle (for three songs) while Lata Mangeshkar too sang a song, and Shamshad Begum's voice was also used in one qawwali. Geeta Dutt's vocals were restricted to only one song: 'Balam se milan hoga', a sweet song that played in the background.

With this movie Geeta stopped singing for Waheeda Rehman altogether. It was clear that she wasn't the lead singer even in her husband's films any longer.

The gossip magazines were all out saying that with the entry of 'rivals' Lata Mageshkar and Asha Bhosle in the 'Guru Dutt camp', Geeta Dutt had lost even at her home turf. The conversations in the industry clearly hinting that her personal life's crisis was affecting her already precarious professional life.

The shooting of *Chaudhvin Ka Chand* was fast progressing. Guru Dutt was aware that to make a successful film, it was crucial to have chart-busting songs. He had handed over the reins of direction to M. Sadiq but he himself was directing the songs of *Chaudhvin Ka Chand*. The music sittings for finalising the lyrics and tunes of the songs were intense. Music composer, Ravi, recalled that Guru Dutt would listen to everyone. Suggestions were welcome. Never did he discourage anyone from coming up with new ideas, even if they opposed his conception.

Ravi said, 'That was a great thing. He always meant what he said. That night, three songs were tuned in fact. Johnny Walker's "Yeh duniya gol hai" and "Mili khaak mein mohabbat" were also created that night. In fact, Guru Dutt liked the last song so much that we sat up the whole night and I must have sung it at least five hundred times then.'

However, music composer Ravi also explained why Asha Bhosle featured prominently in the album. 'Two mujras were to be composed for this film. We, that is, Guru Dutt, Shakti Samanta, writer S.H. Bihari and myself, went to listen to a noted singer in the city. Guru Dutt wanted the typical style and manner of the original mujras and not something filmi. Next day we composed a tune and I played it to him. He asked me gently whether Geeta, his wife, could sing it. I said I would do a riyaz with her and called her up. It was a difficult tune and Geeta had a particular style and limitations of her own. Yet, how could I tell her anything? She herself realised this and even before I could say anything, she rang up Guru Dutt and told him it was a difficult, classical number which she could not do full justice to. Asha Bhosle was finally taken to render it.'

Though Ravi made it sound simplistic, but a singer of Geeta Dutt's calibre admitting she could not do justice to a difficult song sounds unreal today. It seems the decision wasn't taken due to one single reason but a variety of personal as well as professional factors contributed towards it.

The famous Urdu film magazine *Shama*[95] reported, 'Anguished by Guru Dutt's unwillingness to let her sing for other producers combined by his liking for Waheeda Rehman, Geeta Dutt is facing severe depression affecting her personal as well as professional life.'

O.P. Nayyar who produced many evergreen, chartbusters with Geeta had also veered towards Asha Bhosle. 'Geeta said that the turning point in her singing came when O.P. Nayyar began weeding her out as we approached the 1960s. Even more bewildered did she feel by S.D. Burman following suit. She recalled how she had phoned O.P. How she had asked him as to where she had failed him for him no longer to be ringing and asking her to come for a recording.

'Once she called in the middle of the night and said, "Nayyar *saab*, do you still recognize my voice? I am Geeta. *Aap To Humein Bhool Hi Gaye!"* I felt so sad and guilty. That time I could just give her some assurance but it was futile,' recalled O.P Nayyar.[96]

Geeta said that in Nayyar's silence she got her answer.

O.P. Nayyar said later, 'As a singer, she [Asha Bhosle] sang all my songs with her heart and soul. However, Geeta Dutt's voice modulation was far far better. It remains one of my greatest regrets that I phased out Geeta due to my emotional involvement with Asha, when it was Geeta who had introduced me to Guru Dutt. That's when my career really took off.'[97]

Geeta Dutt's singing assignments were shrinking considerably year after year and like Guru Dutt, alcohol and sleeping pills had now become her favourite companions too. The gossips about Guru's personal life had become a regular staple in the industry corridors and it was affecting Geeta badly.

She told writer Bimal Mitra, 'The film magazines, film newspapers are the same. People used to propagate such spicy stories about Guru Dutt and an actress that I was ashamed to read them. I felt like committing suicide… someone wrote your husband was roaming around with a girl. They spent the night together in some hotel…such rumours. Earlier it was not easy to believe. But slowly I felt like believing everything…when I showed those stories to Guru, he would get angry and said I should not read these magazines.'

Two tormented souls living under the same roof. Two talented artists unable to express themselves.

And then a strange incident happened that further deteriorated the relationship.

42

YOU WIN SOME, YOU LOSE SOME

'Director banna tha, director ban gaya; actor banna tha, actor ban gaya; picture achcha banana tha, achche bane. Paisa hai, sab kuch hai, par kuch bhi nahi raha.'

—Guru Dutt

Guru Dutt was in his studio when an envelope bearing his name arrived. Guruswamy had the permission of Guru Dutt to open all work-related envelopes and letters that came to the office. He opened the envelope and was shocked. Inside there was a letter signed by Waheeda Rehman. The letter was personal in nature. It said, 'I want to talk to you about a very personal and crucial matter. Could you please come to Eros at 9 PM tomorrow? I will wait for you. It's really important.'

A shocked Guruswamy took the letter to Guru Dutt who was amused after reading it. He met Waheeda almost every day in the studio. They were shooting the film together. What was the need of writing a letter and asking him to meet at a crowded place like a theatre? The whole thing sounded strange to Guru Dutt. This couldn't be Waheeda! It didn't even look like her handwriting. Was it a prank? He was curious to know who had actually written the letter.

He went near the designated place the next day at 9 PM, and waited there for a while but no one came. He immediately drove down to Geeta's house in Santa Cruz and asked for Geeta. Geeta's mother was shocked to see him so late. She told him that Geeta had come that afternoon but left early. Guru Dutt knew Geeta wasn't at the Pali Hill home. He was furious.

He realised it was Geeta who had sent the letter to verify her suspicions about Guru Dutt and Waheeda and hoping to catch Guru Dutt red-handed.

That night, there was a major confrontation between Geeta and Guru Dutt and both said things they had never said to each other before. According to Abrar Alvi, 'I think this was the first time that night after going home, that he confronted Geeta with the episode and, as he confessed to me later, raised his hand on her.'[98]

This tumultuous incident cracked open the fault lines of the relationship.

After this there was little left to hold on to.

Cameraman V.K. Murthy was back in Bombay and taking him along, Guru Dutt decided to go to Baroda (in Gujarat) to hunt for shooting locations. It was there that Murthy realised that more than the location, it was Guru Dutt's need to escape from the city and from his life which had brought them there.

V.K. Murthy recalled a heartbreaking conversation.

'*Kaagaz Ke Phool* upset him very much, though he didn't express it to others…while scouting for locations in Baroda for *Chaudhvin Ka Chand,* he narrated me a line from *Pyaasa*: "Agar yeh duniya mujhe mil bhi jaye to kya hai."

'I asked him why he said that suddenly. "Mujhe waise hi lag raha hai. Dekho na, mujhe director banna tha, director ban gaya; actor banna tha, actor ban gaya; picture achcha banana tha, achche bane. Paisa hai, sab kuch hai, par kuch bhi nahi raha,"[99] he told me.'[100]

43

THE PHENOMENAL COMEBACK

'He would be struggling to come out of his shell and the surest way to throw him back into it was to ask him, "What's ailing you? Come on! Get it off your chest."'

—Abrar Alvi

Guru Dutt had bought a floor in Modern Studios in the Andheri area in Bombay. He renamed it as Guru Dutt Studios. The major portions of *Chaudhvin Ka Chand* were being shot in this studio.

Film-making was his reverent refuge. The studio his temple. It was in studios, during shootings, that Guru Dutt appeared in control, sometimes shouting for the perfect shot, sometimes cheerfully acting out the scenes for his artists, giving the impression that everything was fine with him, as if he was living his life. No one understood if he truly felt joyous when he was shooting or if this was a facade. Whatever this feeling was, it would vanish by late evenings. Then he would drink with friends and associates, who would be busy having animated conversations with

Dutt chipping in occasionally, smiling once in a while. But he would just be a lonely soul in a crowd.

With alcohol there were always books too. When Guru used to sleep, his man Friday, Ratan, would keep a lot of books and a table lamp near his bed. Perhaps like alcohol, he was looking for some kind of an intoxication in books. Books in Hindi, Urdu, Sanskrit, English and Bengali. His nights were spent with whiskey and words printed on paper.

As the night progressed, he would go silent, lost in his thoughts.

'At times he would come to me late in the night. I knew something was weighing on his mind which he wanted to share with someone. He would be struggling to come out of his shell and the surest way to throw him back into it was to ask him, "What's ailing you? Come on! Get it off your chest,"' wrote Abrar Alvi[101] about Guru Dutt's condition.

Guru Dutt was perhaps living inside a box that was so dark that no one could see his pain, so dark that even he could not see a way out of it.

Guru Dutt's younger brother, Devi Dutt, who was looking after the publicity of the film recalled, 'Initially I was asked to popularise the ghazal "Chaudhvin ka chand ho tum ya aftab ho". I was asked to frequent all the restaurants and Irani joints and to play the song on the jukebox. The ghazal became so popular that everyone used to enquire about the film! Even my friends used to wonder why I kept playing the song every time.'

Director M. Sadiq's detailing of the film's milieu and cultural background was apt. It was the song sequences, directed by Guru Dutt himself which proved to be the highlights of the film. Guru Dutt looked good, Rehman dashing, Johhny Walker was back in his elements after his miscasting in *Kaagaz Ke Phool* and above all, Waheeda looked her best.

With its music already topping the charts, *Chaudhvin Ka Chand* was released in June 1960.

It was undoubtedly a deeply regressive story at every level. In an ideal world, such stories should not even work as a fantasy but the audience who had thrown the proverbial stones at *Kaagaz Ke Phool,* lapped up *Chaudhvin Ka Chand.* It went on to become a monstrous hit.

Two months later, one of the most iconic films of Indian cinema, K. Asif's magnum opus *Mughal-e-Azam* was released and the focus shifted to that film. But *Chaudhvin Ka Chand* continued running to packed houses even with *Mughal-e-Azam* playing in other theaters.

Within just eight months of the box office disaster of *Kaagaz Ke Phool*, Guru Dutt had made a phenomenal comeback. This is an aspect of Guru Dutt that is seldom talked about. It says a lot about Dutt's understanding of the commercial aspect of cinema. In his career, he produced just one flop film through his film production company: *Kaagaz Ke Phool.* And he never forgot that failure. The extraordinary success of *Chaudhvin Ka Chand* not just saved Guru Dutt from financial ruin but commercially it also went on to become Guru Dutt's most successful film ever.

The blockbuster established Waheeda Rehman as one of the top female stars of Hindi cinema. In *Chaudhvin Ka Chand* she looked ethereal, especially in the title song. This was the only film which potrayed a proper romance between Guru Dutt and Waheeda on screen and their chemistry was nothing short of sensual and magical. At that time, colour films had just started being made, and Guru Dutt decided to take the title song of the film, shoot it in colour and re-release it with new fanfare.

'While reshooting the song in colour, they used hard, huge lights directly on my face, and my skin burnt; we had to shoot constantly with ice-packs being applied, and my eyes were red from all the heat. Later, we heard from the Censor Board that the song is very "hot!" and lascivious, which shocked Guru Dutt. He argued it was the same shot, the same movements from last time, only shot in colour! They replied that Waheeda's eyes have turned red. He was bewildered, and said yes, but that happens while shooting, but what does it have to do with anything? They told him that it was very sensual and suggestive! He came back and had a big laugh about it, "Yeh Censor waale!"' remembered Waheeda Rehman.

44

BAFFLED WITH LIFE

'I sometimes wonder why he was so baffled with life!'

—Ravi (music composer)

The success of *Chaudhvin Ka Chand* was great news for his staff too who had stood by him in the worst of times. Their salaries came with a surprise bonus.

Guru Dutt wanted to celebrate his comeback in 'his city'. He decided to go to Calcutta for the premier of the film. But even in the midst of success and celebrations, he wasn't able to hide his inner turmoil. Lalitha Lajmi says, 'Though *Chaudhvin Ka Chand* was a big success, Guru Dutt's personal life was really disturbed and it seemed he was going through full blown depression by then.'

Waheeda Rehman says, 'He would often lapse into spells of silence. While we'd all be gathered around chatting about the latest English films or whatever, he would be sitting by himself, totally lost and away from the world around him. We used to call to him, and he'd "wake" with a start. He'd be thinking about something else, very distracted.'

Music director Ravi recalled, 'He was a very generous man. When in Calcutta for the premiere of *Chaudhvin Ka Chand*, he would give away money so generously to his workers. But he was not keeping well and had started taking drugs.'[102] At the premiere evening he came down from his room wearing a crumpled kurta-pyjama. The team requested him to wear something more formal and finally dressed him in a sherwani. But despite everyone's request he was unable to speak on the premiere day. 'He requested the public that since he was not well, he would not speak. The public was craving to just have a glimpse and he came on stage during the interval for a few minutes, that's all,' said Ravi.

What came next was a promise from Guru Dutt that Ravi never forgot.

'The next day, everyone gathered in my hotel room. He was very happy and said that the film was big hit and all of us deserved a prize. He turned to me and said that the music was a definite winner to make the film such a hit and told me to ask for anything I wanted. I made him promise that, and then asked for his bottle of drugs. He smiled and promised that he would give it to me and stop taking them.'

Then they came back to Bombay and got busy with their respective lives. Ravi wondered, 'When it came to his films, he always knew what was to be done next. He had his priorities right. I sometimes wonder why he was so baffled with life!'

45

SLEEPLESS NIGHTS

'I think I'll go mad!'

—Guru Dutt

For more than a month, Bimal Mitra was in Lonavla with Abrar Alvi working on the story and script of *Sahib Bibi Aur Ghulam*. Mitra used to translate his novel and write the basic draft of the story. Then Abrar would take it over for the screenplay and dialogues. Guru Dutt often visited the farmhouse to see how the script was progressing. In his mind the rule was still clear—an artistic film after every commercial film. He was also happy that *Sahib Bibi Aur Ghulam* was to be shot in Bengal.

Sleep evaded him even at the quiet farmhouse. He would always want someone who could sit with him. It was a person called Ratan who would be there for him at all times. As soon as Guru Dutt would call Ratan he would have to appear and ask, 'What can I get you sir?' Dutt could ask for a cigarette or anything under the sun. Then there was the cook, John. He would prepare a new food menu for Guru Dutt daily. He would eat little but wanted the table to be full.

The title of the book that Bimal Mitra wrote in Bangla about his experiences with Guru Dutt was *Binidra*, meaning 'Sleepless'. This was one aspect of Guru Dutt that finds multiple mentions in the book. It was as if he never slept. They shared a good time together in Lonavala for almost one and a half months. Mitra used to be asleep by midnight. But not Guru. He would be up till 4–5 AM.

One day Mitra asked, 'What is the reason of your sleeplessness?'[103]

Guru Dutt replied, 'I don't know! Some obscure things kept me awake.'

'What obscure things?'

'Conversations about my films, my son and some other vague things keep coming to my mind. Vague things. They really don't mean anything.'

'Before sleeping, why don't you count from 1 to 100?'

'I have done it all.'

'Have you tried sleeping without a pillow?'

'Yes I have.'

'But if you don't sleep the whole night, isn't it painful the next day?'

'Ab to aadat padh chuki hai,'[104] answered Guru Dutt.

Bimal Mitra writes, 'I noticed Guru was very different from others. Despite not sleeping the entire night, he would appear calm and nonchalant. You couldn't gauge what's going on in his mind. But I could see the pain he was going through and the guilt that was growing in his body.'

He would often say, 'Bimal Babu, I think I'll go mad!'

Section Eleven

BUILDING OF A DREAM

1956–57

'Maybe, Guru Dutt saw a muse in Waheeda.'

46

SAILAAB AND *C.I.D.*

> 'Deep-seated within was a tremendous ambition...to be original and different.'
>
> —Dev Anand

While working on *C.I.D.* and *Pyaasa*, Guru Dutt had also realised that success comes with its own sweet price. He was basically a creative person but as the head of his company he was also responsible to make it financially stable. The running cost of the company including the salaries of the staff was Rs 40,000 per month—a huge amount in those times. There were huge concerns about the inflow of the cash and income tax issues that used to tire his creative soul. He was a generous man who used to take great care of his staff.

So much was happening in Guru Dutt's life and career. 'Deep-seated within was a tremendous ambition to fight against the stereotyped, set conventionalism of the early fifties, to be original and different,' remembered Dev Anand. While *C.I.D.* was nearing completion and Guru Dutt was readying for *Pyaasa*, another Guru Dutt-'directed' film released on 13 April 1956.

The film *Sailaab* ('Flood') is always mentioned in Guru Dutt's filmography but is not talked about much. The reason behind this is *Sailaab* wasn't planned by Guru Dutt. It was a film produced by Geeta Dutt's brother, Mukul Roy, who was its music director too. Geeta Dutt decided to help finance the project because of her brother. The film had Geeta Bali, Abhi Bhattacharya and Smriti Biswas in lead roles and the director was Ravindra Dave. During the shooting, Ravindra Dave developed some serious differences with Mukul Roy and left the film midway.

It was a serious moment of crisis and a matter of great concern for Mukul Roy and Geeta. Guru Dutt was requested to take over and complete the film, which he graciously did. He was also credited as the director of *Sailaab*.

In its review, the magazine *Filmindia* blasted *Sailaab* calling it a 'picture for your worst enemy' and 'a perfect instrument of torture' describing it as boring, stupid and incoherent. *Sailaab* is not discussed among the films of Guru Dutt as no print of the film is known to survive. So it can't be critiqued like other popular films of Guru Dutt.

Sailaab was a disaster at the box office. A resounding flop which left both Mukul Roy and Geeta Dutt in financial doldrums. Guru Dutt practically disowned *Sailaab*. Geeta was pregnant and this financial disaster broke her heart. She lost so much money that she had to declare personal bankruptcy and insolvency.

This insolvency also meant that Geeta Dutt could never hold any shares in Guru Dutt Films Pvt. Ltd.

After the *Sailaab* disaster, Guru Dutt needed some good news soon. And that came with *C.I.D.*

Released on 17 August 1956, *C.I.D.* was immediately lapped up by the masses. It was an immensely entertaining crime thriller with Dev Anand playing a suave policeman on a mission to find the killers of a newspaper editor.

According to Raj Khosla, Guru Dutt never interfered in the shooting of *C.I.D.* but visually and thematically, the film maintained the typical Guru Dutt style of an urban crime caper.

Like all Guru Dutt productions, *C.I.D.* too was a musical triumph. O.P. Nayyar and lyricist Majrooh Sultanpuri created songs that have stood the test of time and are still hummable. These include 'Boojh mera kya naam re' sung by Shamshad Begum, 'Ankhon hi ankhon mein ishara ho gaya' sung by Geeta Dutt and Mohammed Rafi, the evergreen 'Ae dil hai mushkil jeena yahan' sung by Mohammed Rafi and picturised on Johnny Walker (hugely 'inspired' by 'My Darling Clementine!'), 'Leke pehla pehla pyar' sung by Shamshad Begum, Asha Bhosle and Mohammed Rafi.

'Kahin pe nigahen kahin pe nishana' and 'Jaata kahan hai deewane' were picturised on the vamp, Waheeda Rehman. 'Jaata kahan hai deewane' had Geeta Dutt in raging form but the song does not find itself into the film. Reportedly, the Censor Board did not approve showing a *C.I.D.* officer being bewitched by a vamp! They also objected to the use of the word 'fifi' ('Kuch mere dil mein fifi, kuch tere dil mein fifi') as it was sounding too suggestive to them. However, Waheeda Rehman said in an interview that it was not the word 'fifi' that caused the problem. It was the line 'Jaata kahan hai deewane, sab kuch yahan hai sanam', which the Censor Board found suggestive. Decades later a remix version of the song was used in Anurag Kashyap's *Bombay Velvet* picturised on Anushka Sharma. The magic of the composition was still intact.

47

MENTOR–PROTÉGÉ

'Although I was the heroine in *C.I.D.*, it was Waheeda who was given a lot of importance because she was a Guru Dutt protégé.'

—Shakila

The second half of 1956 turned out to be exceptional for Guru Dutt. Professionally, *C.I.D.* became the highest grossing film of 1956, earning huge money for Guru Dutt's company and a beaming Guru Dutt gifted Raj Khosla a Dodge convertible for making the smash hit. Khosla recalled, 'He was a tremendously generous person. After *C.I.D.*, one day he called me and just handed me the keys of a car. It was a Dodge convertible. He said: "Here it is, here's your car." "What's this all about?" "It's a present for you for making *C.I.D.*" And the beauty of it was, when I took the car home, I found the paperwork and everything was in my name. I did not have to bother to do anything further.'[105]

There had been celebrations on the personal front too.

A month before *C.I.D.* was released, Guru Dutt's second son, Arun, was born on 10 July 1956.

Raj Khosla never forgot the Calcutta premier of *C.I.D.* There were heavy rains so the flights from Bombay to Calcutta were cancelled. So Guru Dutt and the team decided to go by train. The starcast of *C.I.D.* including Dev Anand and Waheeda Rehman reached Calcutta after a forty-six-hour long train journey. When they reached the theatre, it was a full house. Guru Dutt watched the film for only twenty minutes and told Raj Khosla, 'Come on, Raj, let's go. You've made a super film, let's celebrate.' This was around 10 PM. The celebrations began in the hotel and went on till midnight.

But the next morning, Raj Khosla couldn't find Guru in his hotel suite. He recalled, 'I went looking for him everywhere, and there he was, lying fast asleep in the bathtub, fully dressed, bow tie and all. We had been drinking all night. He was very sweet.'[106]

However, Abrar Alvi remembered the Calcutta premiere in a different context. Hinting at the closeness of Guru Dutt and Waheeda Rehman, he said, 'I think it was during the premiere of *C.I.D.*, in Calcutta, that people started getting an inkling of the budding relationship.'[107]

The film magazines in Bombay had started to talk openly about Guru Dutt's fondness for his new 'discovery'. The people in Guru Dutt's team had also realised that Guru Dutt, who was extremely short-tempered at the shootings and was ready to shout at anyone if proceedings did not go as he wished, became extremely patient when Waheeda Rehman was shooting.

Though Shakeela was the lead actress in the film, it was Waheeda Rehman who was talked about much in her supporting role of the golden-hearted vamp. Being a dancer, she handled the song sequences with amazing grace but her expressions look gauche and awkward for a sultry character. Raj Khosla intelligently focuses on her eyes to get the required effect. Infact during the shooting of *C.I.D.* the unit knew that Guru Dutt had shown great faith in the new girl Waheeda.

Even the lead actress of *C.I.D.*, Shakila, had said, 'Although I was the heroine in *C.I.D.*, it was Waheeda who was given a lot of importance because she was a Guru Dutt protégé.'[108] The film magazines had announced that impressed by Waheeda Rehman, Guru Dutt had given her a crucial role in his most ambitious project *Pyaasa*.

During *C.I.D.*, Raj Khosla wasn't happy with Waheeda's work and attitude and had told Guru Dutt: '*C.I.D.* will be her last film.' But after watching the rushes of the *Pyaasa* song 'Jaane kya tune kahi', Raj was surprised and said, 'How is it possible? She is bad in my film and has done a good job here.'

In the book *Conversations with Waheeda Rehman* by Nasreen Munni Kabir,[109] Waheeda says, 'Guruduttji tried explaining: "Raj, she is very raw; you need to handle her right. May be she did the song well because she is a dancer. She knows how to give silent expressions. She needs a little guidance because she isn't familiar with camera angles. When you use a 75 mm lens, she gets very stiff. You have to make her relax."'

The new mentor-protégé relationship was already being talked about in the corridors of the film industry.

Section Twelve

DESTRUCTION OF A DREAM

1960–63

'I'm not afraid of death but I'm scared for life.'

48

SCARED FOR LIFE

'I find myself unable to stay in that house.'

—Guru Dutt

Waheeda Rehman was shooting in Mahabaleshwar that is around 150 kilometers from Lonavala. After her shoot got over, she came to the the Lonavala farmhouse one day with her sister and brother-in-law. Guru was very happy seeing her there. Everyone ate together. After spending some time at the farmhouse, they left for Bombay.

'After they left I kept on thinking about the connection between Guru Dutt and Waheeda Rehman. From the day I came to Bombay I was hearing things about Waheeda and Guru,' recalled Bimal Mitra.

Guru Dutt told him, 'You don't even meet many people so you have no clue about the extent of these rumours. But so many magazines are spreading rumours and trying to ruin my family life.'

'Yes, I have heard some of these conversations,' said Bimal Mitra.

'But, you know, I always want to remain happy with my family. Of all the houses and buildings in Pali Hill, my home is the most beautiful. When I am in that house, I don't feel I am in Bombay. That garden, that ambience—where else would I get it? But even then I find myself unable to stay in that house.'

It was true that even in the comfort and luxury, Guru Dutt would spar with pain. For Dutt, Bombay meant insomnia. He was sleepless in his palatial house. Of late, things with Geeta had come to a point where he would regularly leave early morning from Pali Hill to his studio in Andheri.

The studio wouldn't even be open by then. Ratan would unlock the door to his room, go inside and turn on the A.C. Guru Dutt would sit quietly on his chair for some time. There used to be absolute silence. After that he would enter the small adjoining chamber. This was his make-up room. A very small room with a nice bed. He would then close the door from inside and spend the whole day sleeping in that lonely, uninhabited isolation of the make-up room.

Finally, it was here that an unusual deep sleep used to come to Guru Dutt's sleep-deprived eyes.

It was around 2 PM. Everyone was busy working on the script in Lonavala. Guru was sitting quietly in one corner of the room. Suddenly they heard a sound of thunder. Guru went up to the window. It was raining. Within moments, his face transformed and was filled with happiness. It was like a child's face who was suddenly given his favourite candy. 'Bimal Babu, it's raining. I don't feel like working now. Let's go,' Guru said excitedly.[110]

Guru Dutt pulled each person present in the room and went out for a drive. It was raining cats and dogs but Guru was ecstatic. He kept driving. Raindrops kept falling on the windscreen. But nothing worried Guru Dutt. He was happy soaking in the beautiful view of wheat fields, of green trees, of mountains and his car running at a smooth speed on the Bombay-Poona highway. While he was on his own trip, Bimal Mitra sitting in his car was terrified. He shouted, 'Please drive slow!!!'

Guru laughed, 'Why? Are you scared?'

The people sitting in his car that day remembered his joy on that rainy afternoon. They came back to the farm. Guru pulled out a few chairs and kept sitting on the verandah watching the rain for hours. 'I have never seen anyone being so happy looking at rain,' wrote Bimal Mitra.

He later told Bimal Mitra, 'Bimal Babu, I'm not afraid of death but I'm scared for life.'

'Scared of what?'

'Fear, not for myself. In our our film business, we have made some money. We have an amount of 19–20 lakhs. But they can vanish in a moment.'

'But why?'

'Our film business is a kind of like gambling. King today…pauper tomorrow. So I am very scared. I have money, fame…I have a family. If all this vanishes one day? You might wonder why do I fear so much despite having so much wealth. I think it is the fear of being alive, the fear of life,' said Guru Dutt.

It was as if Guru was pouring his heart out. Perhaps in his troubled mind, in a twisted way, life might have felt more difficult than death.

Or was he stating a deeper truth—it is harder to live than to die.

49

SAHIB BIBI AUR GHULAM

'During the making of *Sahib Bibi Aur Ghulam*, Geeta and Guru Dutt's fights had increased.'

—Lalitha Lajmi

Finally the script of *Sahib Bibi Aur Ghulam* was ready. This was the first time in Guru Dutt Films Pvt. Ltd that a complete script was ready before the shooting had even begun. Guru Dutt then asked Abrar Alvi to record the entire script in his voice on to a spool. Alvi went to a professional recording studio and recorded the complete script and dialogues with all the emotions and correct intonations. Guru Dutt began to listen to the dialogues repeatedly to imbibe their authentic Urdu flavour. He wanted the film to go on floors very soon.

Everyone expected Guru Dutt to direct the film. He wasn't busy with any other project at the time. But Lalitha Lajmi says he wasn't in the right frame of mind to take up that responsibility. 'The tension in his personal life had increased many fold during *Sahib Bibi Aur Ghulam*. So he gave the chance of direction to Abrar but he directed the songs.'[111] The events that happened during the making of the film proved that his mental state was indeed fragile.

Abrar Alvi recalled an evening in Lonavala where Guru Dutt talked about his decision of not directing *Sahib Bibi Aur Ghulam.* Abrar and actor Ram Singh who was present there tried to reason with him. But Guru Dutt replied, 'The trouble is, Ram Singh, that not only do I know how to direct, I also know what it takes to direct. The mental agony, the emotional fatigue that I am going through is hardly the condition even for a master to be in while directing.'

Initially he thought about giving the directorial reins to Satyen Bose and later to Nitin Bose, but finally decided that his closest associate, writer Abrar Alvi, would direct the film. It was a superb opportunity for Alvi to prove himself as a film-maker. Abrar was sent to Calcutta to understand the Bengali milieu and the background of zamindars.

This was a story Guru Dutt was deeply involved with. Abrar Alvi knew that with great opportunity, a huge weight of expectations had also fallen on his shoulders.

It was now time for casting.

For the pivotal role of 'Chhoti Bahu', Guru Dutt zeroed in on the glamorous Chhaya Arya, the wife of photographer Jitendra Arya. The couple was based in London but Guru Dutt persuaded them to move to Bombay. The couple came to Bombay and a photoshoot was done with Chhaya Arya. She was also made to listen to the script recorded on tape and her dialogue delivery test was done too. But when the stills from the photoshoot arrived, Dutt was disappointed. Chhaya looked too urban with chiselled features. While Dutt wanted a face that had soft 'motherly' features yet appeared wanton in the complex role of Chhoti Bahu. It was particularly crushing for Chhaya who had shifted her base from London only for this film. But as a film-maker, Guru Dutt didn't compromise. It was only the film that counted.

Shashi Kapoor was the first choice to play Bhootnath. But reportedly he turned up two and a half hours late. Guru Dutt was irritated and said, 'If he's late by almost three hours for a narration what will happen later?' Then Biswajeet was offered the role but he backed out too. Finally, Guru Dutt himself became Bhootnath.

Waheeda Rehman, a prominent star by then, wanted to play Chhoti Bahu. She even did a look test and photoshoot wearing a Bengali sari. But the photographs did not please Guru Dutt. He felt Waheeda looked too young for the role that demanded a mature actress. 'Tu to chuha lag rahi hai,'[112] Guru Dutt told Waheeda laughingly, but offered her the role of the pesky Jaba who got to sing 'Bhanwara bada nadan hai' in the film.[113]

However, Abrar Alvi was of the opinion that Waheeda

was miscast even for the role of Jaba. According to Alvi, Waheeda's personality wasn't suited for the role of a mischievous girl with a mercurial temperament. But Guru Dutt was keen on casting her, and Waheeda too consented despite being aware of the fact that this wasn't the main heroine's part but a second lead. Alvi says, 'Meanwhile, the relationship between the two had blossomed and Guru Dutt was very possessive of her and kept directing her through the scenes.'[114]

Lalitha Lajmi says, 'During the making of *Sahib Bibi Aur Ghulam*, Geeta and Guru Dutt's fights had increased. He was deeply involved with his film but Geeta used to suspect all the time. An artist needs space.'

So much has been written about the Guru Dutt-Waheeda Rehman association/alleged relationship, but Guru Dutt's closest associate, Abrar Alvi, had himself spilled the beans in author Sathya Saran's book, *Ten Years with Guru Dutt*: 'Many of us in the unit felt that Waheeda was infinitely more suitable as a partner for Guru Dutt than his wife Geeta. Guru Dutt's mother too shared our opinion…he would pack up shooting at any time without provocation, and make any excuse to be alone with her, even sending me away. Often he would say to me, "I do not know why I cannot overwhelm her…" And that from as private a man as he, was as good as a declaration of involvement.'

In *Conversations with Waheeda Rehman* by Nasreen Munni Kabir, Nasreen directly asks: 'There continues to be much speculation about your relationship with him. Everyone assumed that you were in love with each other. Did that cause a scandal when you were making films with him?'

To this, Waheeda answers: 'Because his death was a mystery—no one knew for sure whether it was a suicide or an accident—there was much curiosity. His death was such a shock to us all. He was only thirty-nine. He was young. The question everyone asked was: "Why did he have to die like that?" None of my film colleagues have ever asked me personal questions about our relationship. It was always other people and the press who were curious, and still are, almost sixty years later.

'I know we're public figures, but I strongly believe my private life should remain private. What ultimately matters and concerns the world is the work we leave behind,' said Waheeda Rehman.

50

ART IMITATES LIFE

'*Sahib Bibi Aur Ghulam* is the story of our lives.'

—Geeta Dutt

1 January 1961, the shooting of *Sahib Bibi Aur Ghulam* began with an auspicious muhurat ceremony. The first shot was being canned. Bimal Mitra was invited again from Calcutta to grace the momentous occasion. Guru Dutt had shaved his trademark moustache to play Bhootnath. He appeared super excited. Then there was Waheeda Rehman who was playing the character of the Bengali girl, Jaba. Waheeda was wearing a traditional Bengali sari. But there was another big surprise in store for everyone during the lunch. The crew at the Guru Dutt studios saw Guru Dutt, Geeta Dutt and Waheeda Rehman eating together.

A curious Bimal Mitra asked Geeta, 'Hello! Good to see you. Never seen you in the studio before?'

'The film was being launched today, so I came,' replied Geeta.

Guru Dutt interrupted, 'No, I have called Geeta.

Waheeda didn't know how to tie a Bengali style sari, so I asked Geeta to tell her.'

'How am I looking?' asked Waheeda.

'Very good.'

'Am I looking like a Bengali girl?'

'Hundred per cent!' replied Bimal Mitra.

The women were referring to each other as Geeta Ji and Waheeda Ji. Post lunch, Guru and Waheeda left for the shot. Bimal Mitra and Geeta were left alone at the table.

Mitra asked Geeta, 'How did you like the shooting?'

Geeta replied, 'It was good! There was a time when I had asked him not to make this film.'

'Why?'

'Because, *Sahib Bibi Aur Ghulam* is the story of our lives.'

The next seven days Guru Dutt was neck-deep into shooting. He was trying hard to distract himself from the fire of unrest and restlessness burning in his mind.

And then a tragedy struck.

On 22 January 1961, Guru Dutt's father, Shivashankar Padukone, passed away suddenly. He used to live with Guru Dutt at the Pali Hill bungalow. Lalitha Lajmi remembers, 'Father was ok that morning. Guru Dutt had gone for work as usual. But as soon as the news reached him, he came back and was furious at our family doctor, Dr Robero. He was so angry that he had a fight with the doctor as he thought father died because of some allergic reaction due to wrong medication. Guru Dutt said he would take the doctor to court.'[115] No one was prepared for his sudden death but Guru Dutt particularly took it badly. He couldn't bear to be in Bombay. After the last rites, Guru Dutt left for Lonawala.

In the later years Guru had not spent much time with his father owing to his work and personal life. 'Father was a self-contained, talented man who pursued literature but was bored by the pursuit of worldly success.' While growing up, Guru resented his father's lack of enterprise. It was after his father was gone that Guru Dutt realised that in his worldview, he was similar to his father. He wrote, 'It was years later that I realised that worldly success is not so important.' His life's dichotomy was strange—he wanted to rule the world of movies and at the same time he wanted to run away from this world.

Already dealing with personal turmoil, the death of his father was too traumatic for him. He visited the Haji Malang dargah (shrine) looking for peace and answers to his pain.[116]

'Sometimes he used to say that an astrologer had predicted that he would go mad at the age of thirty-two and he believed it,' shared Guru Dutt's younger brother, Atmaram, in Nasreen Munni Kabir's book *Guru Dutt: A Life in Cinema*.

He further added, 'I think it really was true. He had started drinking heavily, but never when he was shooting. He was a strict disciplinarian as far as work was concerned, but totally undisciplined in his personal life.'

Not just the mental condition, but his physical condition was also worsening. All the alcohol and those sleeping pills were taking their toll on his nerves and liver. His family doctor, Dr Robero, gave him regular injections. Guru hated them. The doctor repeatedly told him to quit both drinking and smoking. Guru Dutt laughed. A sad laughter. Then he said, 'Doctor, you know everything about my life and even then you are telling me to quit whiskey. Yeh jo main abhi bhi zinda hoon, yehi bohot badi baat hai…that I am still alive is a big thing.'

51

SECOND SUICIDE ATTEMPT

'Studio ke darwaaze aur ghar ke darwaaze mein jitna faasla rakhoge, sukhi rahogey. Nahi to ghar mein kaam ki baatein hongi aur studio mein ghar ki baatein hongi.'

—Johnny Walker

The accounts of most of Guru Dutt's close friends suggest that during the making of *Sahib, Bibi aur Ghulam*, Guru Dutt and Geeta had grown further apart. They had realised that their marriage was not working. Geeta Dutt too had taken to alcohol and sleeping pills majorly and left the Pali Hill bungalow to live in his mother's house.

While Geeta had left the house, the corridors of the film studios and film magazines in Bombay were having a field day blaming Waheeda Rehman as the reason of discord between Guru and Geeta. The gossip mills were churning regular columns about their alleged relationship.

According to Abrar Alvi, it was a cause of much concern for Waheeda's mother. She once had this conversation with Abrar, 'Abrar, what will happen to my daughter? My daughter is not the type to flit from man to man, and he is a married man…she tells me that he says he will give up his life for her.'[117]

And then a crazy thing happened.

In author Sathya Saran's book, Abrar Alvi narrates this strange incident. According to Alvi, Waheeda Rehman's brother-in-law, Rauf (Waheeda's elder sister, Sayeeda's husband) made an announcement after the Friday namaz at the Jama Masjid in Bombay. Rauf declared publicly, 'Listen my friends, there's good news. The famous director Guru Dutt is going to become a Muslim and marry my sister-in-law, Waheeda.'[118]

Guru Dutt was in panic. He felt deep embarrassment. He called his close friends Johnny Walker, Rehman and Abrar Alvi to handle Rauf. Somehow the situation was salvaged.

Johnny Walker used to say, 'Studio ke darwaaze aur ghar ke darwaaze mein jitna faasla rakhoge, sukhi rahogey. Nahi to ghar mein kaam ki baatein hongi aur studio mein ghar ki baatein hongi. Tum confuse ho jaaoge ki tum aa rahe ho ya ja rahe ho.[119] And you'll pay a price for it and it's very very costly. Nobody can afford it.'

It was a relief that when this incident happened Geeta Dutt was in London. But Guru Dutt was hurt. He had always been intensely private. He never discussed his personal life in public. He was perhaps scared that things will go out of his hands.

The shooting of *Sahib Bibi Aur Ghulam* continued. He shot his scenes with Waheeda. Though Abrar was directing the film, he was also keenly involved in the shooting process. For the songs, Guru Dutt took the mantle. But no one really knew what was going on in his mind.

Then one night, Guru Dutt swallowed thirty-eight sleeping pills. It was his second attempt at suicide.

52

THE BIG DECISION

> 'We called a psychiatrist but he charged Rs 500 for a visit. My brother Atma laughed that he is just talking with Guru and he is so expensive. We never called him again.'
>
> —Lalitha Lajmi

'It was an overdose of sleeping pills. We rushed him to Nanavati Hospital but his condition was very serious. His body had gone completely cold. He was unconscious for three days. Then on the fourth day we heard his scream. My brother was shouting. The first person he asked for was Geeta. It was strange because their relationship was going through hell. They were thinking of separation but in those moments, he wanted Geeta to be near him. I think they deeply loved each other despite their major differences.' recalled Lalitha Lajmi.

Lalitha believed this suicide attempt had been pre-planned. Guru Dutt had even written a letter for his brother Atmaram in which he asked Atmaram to take care of Geeta and his kids and look after the studio and Guru Dutt Films.

It was personally very traumatic for Lalitha too. She went into depression and had to take medication for a long time. But she says Guru Dutt never talked about the reason why he tried to end his life. 'Sometimes if there was an altercation with Geeta he used to call me. I would rush to him even in the middle of the night. But he would sit quietly, not say anything. I felt he wanted to say something. But he never did. Never.'

A person who attempted suicide twice yet never talked about it with his family. It was as if through these suicide attempts, Guru Dutt was crying for help. On the doctor's suggestion, the family called a psychiatrist for counselling. 'I was much younger than him and in those days no one really talked about such things. We also called a psychiatrist but he charged Rs 500 for a visit. My brother Atma laughed that he was just talking with Guru and he is so expensive. We never called him again,' said Lalitha, adding that sometimes she blames herself for not doing enough for her brother.

Guru came back from the hospital and in a few days the shooting was resumed as if nothing had happened. The team was happy to see him back at the studio.

But apperently there were numerous other times that Guru Dutt experimented with sleeping pills.

Screenwriter Nabendu Ghosh recounts, 'Let me tell you about a doctor whose name was A.J. Ribero, a very stubborn man. He was an MBBS, and a sweet-spoken doctor, who had [his] clinic in Santa Cruz. Ribero was a general physician. Because of Ribero's goodwill, all affluent people of Santa Cruz, Khar and Bandra would visit him. Especially all those who were associated with films. Famous film personalities like Filmistaan's Shashadhar Mukherjee, director Aurobindo Sen, Shakti Samanta, etc. Guru Dutt was no exception. I have already said how I often visited Guru Dutt's Pali Hill home for discussions. One morning, I reached his house and found out that the situation was tense. I saw Dr Ribero, going inside the bedroom and coming out every two or three minutes with a tense look on his face. I asked, "What's up, doctor?" Dr Ribero said, "Guru took sleeping pills, he's still not coming back to his senses, I have been trying for half an hour, Geeta is crying." But about five minutes later, Dr Ribero came out of the room, sat down on the chair and said, "Thank god, he's now conscious." Then again one day, about three months later, I saw a similar situation at their house. I asked Dr Ribero, "Now what has happened?" Ribero said, "Today Debi [Geeta] is unconscious. She took a lot of sleeping pills. Guru is sitting quietly. I will wait for another ten minutes. If she doesn't recover, I'll be forced to call the police." But five minutes later, Geeta came back to her senses.'

'The news may not have reached you. I tried to commit suicide,' Guru Dutt once told Bimal Mitra.

Though Guru Dutt explained his reasons citing his father's demise, some income tax problem, and certain other disturbing personal episodes. Mitra just kept looking at his face. This was a man who had attempted suicide and eventually survived. Now hearing the story of his experience of attempted suicide sounded surreal, unnatural, and unbelievable.

'So what did you do that day?'

'A tube contains thirty-eight tablets. I dissolved all of them in water and drank.'

Guru added that there is no rational reason for the torture that his life has been going through for the last few years. He said all the events are happening only after his father's death. There is a lot of unrest...and a lot of wealth as well. 'Who gives so much turmoil? And why is so much money coming? Nowadays, I often wonder what unrest was this...what was the restlessness that I was hell-bent on committing suicide? When I think about this, I get terrorised with fear. But that day, I felt no dilemma in swallowing those sleeping pills.'

But now, after going through this traumatic experience he perhaps wanted to get his life back on track.

But the decision Guru Dutt took, surprised everyone.

53

AND THEN, WAHEEDA LEFT!

'He never offered me another role after *Sahib Bibi Aur Ghulam*.'

—Waheeda Rehman

By late 1961, Abrar Alvi had completed most of the shooting of the film *Sahib Bibi Aur Ghulam* except for the role of Chhoti Bahu. The scenes of Waheeda Rehman were also shot. For years, the sets and studio of Guru Dutt Films Pvt. Ltd. had been home for Waheeda. She was a crucial part of the team. She even had a personal make-up room in the studio. But now, one fine morning, she wasn't allowed to enter the make-up room. This happened again the next day.

Without any explanation, Guru Dutt had decided to end his association with Waheeda Rehman. This was perhaps done to give a final chance to his relationship with Geeta.

Some film magazines also said that disturbed by the speculations of their relationship, it was Waheeda Rehman who decided to end her association with Guru Dutt. But neither she nor Guru Dutt ever talked about the episode. Her work in the film had been completed and she stopped coming to the studio.

In Nasreen Munni Kabir's *Conversations with Waheeda Rehman*, Waheeda says, 'It must have been in 1961 or 1962. I don't remember the exact date, but it was during the filming of the final scene in *Sahib Bibi*. Jabba is waiting for Bhoothnath in a carriage in the haveli ruins. That was the last time we worked together. He never offered me another role after *Sahib Bibi*.'

Geeta and Guru Dutt patched up. They even went for a holiday to Kashmir with their two sons, Tarun and Arun. For some time they did seem like a happy family. Geeta was soon pregnant with their third child.

In March 1962, Guru Dutt called Bimal Mitra again to Bombay. This time Guru Dutt asked him to bring his wife too. During this visit, Mitra saw Guru and Geeta happy together. Eating and laughing with each other. They discussed the shooting of *Sahib Bibi Aur Ghulam*. Guru Dutt gave him the good news that super-star Meena Kumari was finally playing the role of Chhoti Bahu; and as it was for the world to see later, she was truly outstanding in the film. Guru was bursting with excitement when he said that producers now wanted him as a lead actor in their films. He even talked about the director of *Mughal-e-Azam*, K.

Asif, who wanted to cast him in his next magnum opus: *Love and God.*

It was difficult to look beyond Guru Dutt's enthusiasm and know what was really going on in his mind. The next few days went like a dream. The families of Guru Dutt and Bimal Mitra went out for long drives and spent a few days in the Lonavala house. Guru's mother also went to Lonavala and told Mitra that it was after a long time that she had seen Guru Dutt laughing.

But the happiness didn't last long.

By the end of March, Mitra was planning to go back to Calcutta. Daily, Geeta would prepare the breakfast and they would eat together. But that morning, a strange silence hung in the air inside the bungalow. Soon they realised that Guru and Geeta had been fighting. An angry Geeta had left late in the night for her mother's house. Mitra's wife went to meet Geeta at her mother's home in Santacruz and came back with a shocking news.

Geeta had tried to end her life by cutting her wrist veins with a blade.

Guru Dutt went to meet Geeta. She said she'll come back when she starts feeling better. Guru was sad and silent. He came back alone and got busy with work.

Sahib, Bibi Aur Ghulam was almost completed but director Abrar Alvi realised that for the last scene, Waheeda Rehman's presence was required. The task of convincing Waheeda was left to Abrar himself.

According to Abrar, Waheeda initially had reservations about coming back to shoot with Guru Dutt.

'Waheeda and Guru Dutt had almost parted and she did not want to come for shooting of the carriage scene in *Sahib Bibi Aur Ghulam*...perhaps it was after this incident l had visited him and for the first time he told me do not keep in touch with her any more,' Lalitha Lajmi told this author.

Waheeda Rehman finally relented with certain conditions. She would not talk to Guru Dutt, they would not touch each other and they would have no dialogues. Abrar agreed.

On the designated day, Waheeda arrived, gave her shot. She did not interact with Guru Dutt at all.

Then Waheeda Rehman left.

54

CHHOTI BAHU

A desperate Guru Dutt had completed the entire shooting of *Sahib Bibi Aur Ghulam* by 1962 except for the part that needed the character of Chhoti Bahu. In a memorable passage, Meena Kumari's biographer, Vinod Mehta, narrates how she finally accepted the role that came to define her.

'Negotiations with Meena Kumari were resumed and this time they were more successful. Forty-five clear and consecutive days were offered and the fee raised by 25 per cent.'[120]

Sahib Bibi Aur Ghulam was a dark story of the decline of a Bengali feudal family. The personal story of the family depicting the disintegration of the old zamindar families—the landlords in Bengal and the rise of a new social class in the late 19th century.

The film opens at the ruins of an old haveli in Calcutta, where a group of labourers are busy pulling down what remains of the structure. When the workers break off for lunch, the overseer (Guru Dutt) wanders through the haveli.

As he sits at a place, there begins a flashback to the end of the 19th century. Abrar Alvi, Dutt's screenwriter, is credited with directing it. Officially, Dutt produced the film and directed its song sequences. Yet, the film is quintessential Guru Dutt, imbued as it is with his poetic sensibility, romantic melancholia and unique visual style.

Meena Kumari was devastated on losing the part of Paro in Bimal Roy's *Devdas* to Suchitra Sen. For years, she'd been yearning to play a typical Bengali bahu and finally got her chance. Glass in hand, pallu trailing the floor, kohl-lined eyes reflecting her anguish—she made for a finely imprinted memory. That year, she was the only actress up for Best Actress at the coveted Filmfare Awards with two other nominations apart from *Sahib Bibi Aur Ghulam—Aarti* and *Main Chup Rahungi*.

An enduring saga of decaying feudalism with a parallel sub-plot of the downward-spiral of a zamindar's neglected wife, loaded with unforgettable performances, lilting music, Bhanu Athaiya's costumes, Biren Naug's art direction and V.K. Murthy's cinematography have made this film an unforgettable gem.

Guru Dutt had also wanted S.D. Burman and Sahir Ludhianvi for the music and lyrics, but Burman was unwell and Sahir declined the offer. In walked Hemant Kumar and Shakeel Badayuni on their second project after the mega hit *Bees Saal Baad*, released earler that very year. Hemant Kumar's baton had Geeta Dutt rendering 'Koi door se awaaz de chale aao', 'Piya aiso jiya' and 'Na jao saiyan' for Chhoti Bahu, plus his melancholic background music evoked looming tragedy.

Geeta Dutt didn't playback for Waheeda in this film although in *Pyaasa* she sang for both Mala and Waheeda. Guru Dutt used Asha Bhosle's voice for Waheeda and Geeta sang for Meena Kumari. Amazingly Waheeda Rehman was was not happy with the rushes of the song 'Bhanwara bada nadan hai' and had Guru Dutt reshoot the song. And it was only this ditty from the film which went up to number thirteen on the annual list of Binaca Geetmala in 1962.

55

HAPPINESS AT LAST

'I don't care even if no one watches my film, even if I lose millions. I don't care. But I will not change the climax of my film.'

—Guru Dutt

Initial audience reactions for *Sahib Bibi Aur Ghulam* were not all positive. There were some scenes that the audiences were not liking. The second day Guru Dutt himself went to the Minerva theatre in Bombay to gauge the public reaction. There was a beautiful climax scene which showed Chhoti Bahu resting her head in Bhootnath's lap as they travel in a carriage. The ambiguity about the relationship between Chhoti Bahu and Bhoothnath was taken by the public as a 'relationship' or 'physical desire' between the two.

There was one more scene where Chhoti Bahu asks for one last sip of alcohol. Guru Dutt also realised that the last song 'Sahil ki taraf' was slowing down the narrative.

An indecisive Guru Dutt went straight to K. Asif's house.

Asif asked, 'How's the box office report?'

'Not bad, but not good either,' said Guru.

'Change the climax to comedy. It will run.'

'But how do I make it a comedy?' said Guru Dutt.

'Listen, say in the end Chhoti Bahu has stopped drinking. She is fine now. Everything is good between husband and wife and they live happily ever after,' K. Asif suggested.[121]

Guru came out of his house and called his team in panic mode. Abrar Alvi and Bimal Mitra were asked to write a new climax. Meena Kumari was requested for a day's shoot. Abrar reportedly wasn't convinced but Guru was not listening.

They began writing a new scene when a worried Guru Dutt appeared the next evening and said, 'No, Bimal Babu, I have thought about it. I will not change the film's end.'

Everyone was startled.

He continued, 'I don't care even if no one watches my film, even if I lose millions. I don't care. But I will not change the climax of my film. This film…its climax, it can't really be changed. It's a different kind of a story. It is public's loss if they don't understand it, not mine.'

He added, 'Whatever K. Asif says, I am also a filmmaker, I have my own mind and intelligence. I will not change the end at any cost. Never.'

This was vintage Guru Dutt.

Guru Dutt finally decided to remove the sequence which showed Chhoti Bahu resting her head in Bhootnath's lap as well as the climactic song. Hemant Kumar went on to recycle the tune for 'Sahil ki taraf' for the song 'Ya dil ki suno' in *Anupama* (1966). The song was replaced with a dialogue exchange between Chhoti Bahu and Bhoothnath in the doomed carriage. The new scenes were inserted into every print that was running in theatres.

Guru Dutt later wrote about it:[122]

'I must say the press hailed this attempt with an acclaim which was beyond my expectations. The public reaction was also very encouraging as a whole. In its early screenings at Bombay there was an uproar against only two particular scenes. The first of these was the one in which Chhoti Bahu, out of affectionate affinity between them, rests her head on the lap of Bhoothnath. The second one was the scene in which she tells her husband, "Allow me to take the last sip of liquor. Only for the last time. I have decided to give it up completely." We deleted those scenes.'

The night before the reviews and reports were expected in newspapers, Guru Dutt couldn't sleep. He called his close associates from the team early in the morning. When they reached, Guru was surrounded by a heap of newspapers: English, Hindi, Gujarati, Marathi. Every newspaper. *The Times of India* had declared it 'A classic in celluloid'. A soft smile appeared in Guru Dutt's eyes.

The review in *The Times of India* (24 June 1962) said, 'Within the framework of commercial cinema, *Sahib Bibi Aur Ghulam* is an excellent film...the well-knit screenplay, achieving an effective balance between the various characters and emotional phases, provides a neat dramatic pattern. It appears to be a specially successful job considering the verbosity and digressiveness of the novel of Mr Bimal Mitra who, though often brilliant, writes in a highly disorderly way.'

Then each member started reading the newspapaers out aloud. Ratan and driver Ram Singh were from Gujarat. They began reading the reports in Gujarati newspapers. Guru Dutt was smiling, quietly absorbing the praise.

He praised Abrar Alvi for making a wonderful film. Everyone noticed how happy and cheerful Guru Dutt was that day. There was appreciation coming from all over. That always mattered to him a lot.

That night the thirty-eight-year-old Guru Dutt slept peacefully after a long long time.

56

ESCAPE ROUTES

'Even if I die nobody will mind. Is there anyone objecting to my death?'

—Guru Dutt

Sahib Bibi Aur Ghulam went on to win Filmfare Awards for Best Film, Best Director, Best Actress and Best Photography. The film won the President's Silver Medal and the 'Film of the Year' Award from the Bengal Film Journalist Association and was screened at the Berlin Film Festival in June 1963, also was India's fourth official entry to the Oscars that year, and was nominated for the Golden Bear at the Berlin Film Festival. The celluloid magic of *Sahib Bibi Aur Ghulam* from which even younger masters like Anurag Kashyap and Tigmanshu Dhulia have drawn from!

There was more good news on the personal front.

19 August 1962, Guru and Geeta's third child was born. They named her Nina. Guru always wanted a daughter and was immensely happy. He went to Beirut in Lebanon in October 1962, almost four months after the release of *Sahib*

Bibi Aur Ghulam. From there he wrote a letter to Geeta that was published in the book *Yours Guru Dutt: Intimate Letters of a Great Indian Filmmaker*.[123] In the letter he is talking about the kids and ends with 'love and kisses' and 'Ever yours Guru Dutt'. The letter suggests that things had improved between Guru and Geeta. Although his mother Vaasanthi wrote, 'A girl was born to them. The couple's wish was fulfilled. But alas, peace and harmony became once again unthinkable. The same unpleasantness was repeated.'

Meanwhile, there were more films being offered to him as a lead actor. The biggest film he signed was K. Asif's *Love and God* based on the epic romantic tale of Laila and Majnu. K. Asif was the legendary director who had made the epic film of Indian cinema *Mughal-E-Azam*. Signing Guru Dutt in his next film was a big proof of Guru Dutt's acceptance as a lead actor.

The other outside productions in which Guru Dutt worked as an actor were mostly South Indian productions produced in Madras. The Madras producers were very organised. They made the films quickly and offered good money to Bombay actors. Guru Dutt was working on films like *Bahurani* with Mala Sinha, *Bharosa* with Asha Parekh, *Suhagan* with Mala Sinha again and *Saanjh aur Savera*, a Hrishikesh Mukherjee film with actress Meena Kumari.

Guru Dutt wanted to be away from Bombay and the shootings in Madras came as a huge relief.

He used to say whenever he visited Madras, he felt better and even gained a few pounds that he lost as soon as he was back in Bombay. But was he happy with the kind of films he was working in as an actor? 'Don't ask me about it. I am not satisfied with acting in such films. I act in such films only for money. They pay me a lot of money. Whatever I earn from these films, I use it all to run my studio,'[124] said Guru Dutt.

He also thought about shifting to Calcutta, his soul city. He wished to make Bengali films. He got information that M.P. studio in Calcutta was available for sale. Guru Dutt wanted to buy it. He was even thinking about making staff quarters in the studio and shift his entire staff there. Guruswamy and other members of the staff were baffled. They thanked the almighty when the Madras films happened and Guru Dutt forgot all about buying the Calcutta studio.

But was it really about Madras or Calcutta? Or Guru Dutt just wanted to run away from Bombay? An escape from the city, studio, family life. To anywhere.

He couldn't sleep in Bombay. His constant refrain was: 'I think I will go crazy.'

Lalitha Lajmi says, 'Later he went into depression then slowly his entire personality went down. He kept to himself and became very lonely.'

In Madras, there would be regular addas in Guru's suite. Friends would eat, drink and play cards with Guru in the hotel room. During one of the trips to Madras with Guru Dutt, Bimal Mitra was angry when he saw Guru losing money in a card game. When he told Guru he had been conned, he replied, 'It is good to have some loss. It's not right to make only profit in life.'

Mitra told him that his sleeplessness, heavy dependence on alcohol and sleeping pills can cause severe health issues.

Guru Dutt replied, 'What will happen? I'll die. Listen, even if I die nobody will mind. Is there anyone objecting to my death? If I feel tortured, is it going to harm anyone?'

He was too drunk to talk sense. But even in that state, sleep was evasive.

57

BEGINNING OF THE END

'Guru Dutt was clearly heading towards turning into a mental and physical wreck. I instinctively knew that it was the beginning of the end.'

—B.R. Chopra (Producer/Director)

Since long Guru Dutt had wanted to make a film based on the 1937 film *President* directed by Nitin Bose. When he finally decided to make it, he named it *Baharen Phir Bhi Aayengi.* Guru Dutt asked Shahid Lateef to direct the film. The last film Lateef had directed was the 1958 hit film *Sone Ki Chidiya.* But since five years he hadn't made any other film. Shahid Lateef was also the husband of famous Urdu writer Ismat Chughtai.

O.P. Nayyar made a successful comeback in Guru Dutt Films. He composed memorable songs including the title track, written by poet Kaifi Azmi, and a chartbuster romantic song—'Aapke haseen rukh pe', written by Anjaan and sung by Mohammed Rafi. Guru Dutt filmed it in his distinctive style. The shooting was going on well and the film's release was planned in 1964.

But on the personal front things now simply spiraled downwards.

Sahib Bibi Aur Ghulam was India's offical entry at the 13th Berlin International Film Festival. In June 1963, Guru Dutt, Abrar Alvi and Waheeda Rehman attended the festival. It was after more than a year that Guru and Waheeda came face to face. But according to Abrar Alvi they hardly exchanged a word. The screening happened but the film failed to create any flutter as the international audience could not relate with the overt melodrama and very Indian theme. But something else happened.

Famous journalist and writer on Hindi film music, Raju Bharatan, writes in his book *A Journey Down Melody Lane*: 'As for Waheeda Rehman, she was on her own Berlin trip, with something else on her mind. She, for her own reasons, had decided conclusively yet gracefully to banish Guru Dutt from her life. The last thing Waheeda wanted was a scene, off the sets, in India. She thus waited until the two were in Berlin, where she finally chose to tell her Guru, most emphatically, that they were through.'[125]

'Yes. The last time I saw him must have been in Berlin,' confirmed Waheeda Rehman.

According to Raju Bharatan, *Sahib Bibi Aur Ghulam*'s

outright rejection, coupled with Waheeda's royal rebuff, dealt a body blow to Guru Dutt. Raju Bharatan also quotes the legendary filmmaker B.R. Chopra who was also in Berlin. Bharatan writes, 'The redoubtable B.R. Chopra pulled no punches as he told me: "That man, Guru Dutt, drank all the way back from Berlin to Bombay while keeping all to himself in a corner seat. We knew all about Waheeda having told him, pointblank that she had made up her mind about him and that was it. She also discreetly, left Guru Dutt to find his own way back. Guru Dutt was clearly heading towards turning into a mental and physical wreck. I instinctively knew that it was the beginning of the end.'

Back in Bombay, Geeta had started blaming the bungalow for their deteriorating relationship. Someone had suggested to her that the rift in their relationship began after they shifted to that bungalow. In desperation, she took it seriously. Lalitha recalls,[126] 'She believed that the bungalow was huanted. There was a particular tree in the house and she said there's a ghost in that tree who is bringing bad omen and ruining their marriage. She also had something against a Buddha statue that was kept in their huge drawing room.' According to Lalitha, it was Geeta who said that they should leave the bungalow and live somewhere else. This prospect was heartbreaking for Guru Dutt. After all, it was his dream house.

Section Thirteen

BUILDING OF A DREAM

1957–58

'Of all the houses and buildings in Pali Hill, my home is the most beautiful.'

58

BUNGALOW NO. 48, PALI HILL

'For years I had nutured a dream of building a house in Pali Hill.'

—Guru Dutt

It was a sprawling bungalow of about three bighas of land surrounded by beautiful dense trees and gardens. Guru Dutt's dream home.

In the 1950s, Pali Hill in Mumbai's Bandra (West) suburb was forested with dense undergrowth. Situated on a rolling hill with alternate steep and shallow sides, it garnered the name Pali Hill, although more than one hill is present. In the Pali Hill of early 1950s, most people lived in cottages or bungalows. The bungalows initially were owned by the British, Parsis and the Catholics. Later, film stars such as Dilip Kumar, Dev Anand and Meena Kumari started moving into these properties. They perhaps took a liking to the place because of the greenery and the anonymity it provided. With time Pali Hill grew into an affluent neighbourhood.

Guru Dutt's childhood was marred by financial struggles of the family. The troubles never seemed to end. 'We never had a proper home as kids. During our childhood our house was extremely small and the family was huge. Our father never really could afford any luxuries,' says Lalitha.

Home had eluded him so much that even the idea of a home appeared like a distant dream. 'For years I had nutured a dream of building a house in Pali Hill,' said Dutt. His friend, Dev Anand, had become a star and used to live in a bungalow in Pali Hill. Guru Dutt as a struggling director, used to visit Dev's house often. They were finally working together on a film. During these visits Guru started thinking that if someday he had the means to do it, he would build his own bungalow in Pali Hill. That would be his home. A dream home.

One day Guru Dutt noticed an advertisement in the newspaper about an old bungalow that was going to be sold in Pali Hill. Dutt bought it at Rs 1 lakh, a huge amount in those times. Bungalow No. 48, Pali Hill: Guru Dutt's dream now had a real address. It was a sprawling bungalow situated on about three bighas of land. There were beautiful dense trees and a garden, standing gracefully in the middle of the plush bungalow. Guru and Geeta spend a good bit of time and money designing the home to be unique to their family. Carpets from London, pure Italian marble was ordered for the bathroom, wood was ordered from Kashmir for the roof.

'The bungalow at Pali Hill was shaped into a beautiful house with a big garden, and a lawn in front. From upstairs, the whole area looked lovely on the western side from where the sea and sunset could be seen. He bought different kinds of dogs, lovely birds, a siamese cat, two pairs of hares, a monkey and even a tiger cub. He wanted to start a poultry farm…,' recalled Guru Dutt's mother.

After his second son Arun was born, Guru Dutt and the family moved from their flat in Khar Road to this huge bungalow in Pali Hill. Guru and Geeta were surrounded by happiness. Two kids, success and dreams of a happy life together.

It smelled like home.

But when he had finally realised his dream, very soon he also understood the aching reality that a house is not always necessarily a home. This realisation was the worst part of the dream.

The bungalow was a witness to hundreds of story and shoot planning sessions and musical evenings,. 'Guru Dutt loved classical music. He once invited Akhtari Bai to his residence and only music lovers were invited for the concert,' his mother remembered. He was very fond of animals. Close friends Johnny Walker and Abrar Alvi remembered the times when Guru Dutt summoned them to his bungalow. Alvi talked about the nights when he was woken up to be summoned to Guru Dutt's side to watch with him as fluffy, yellow chickens hatched out of their eggs placed in an incubator by the curious director himself. He would keep observing them for hours.

His mother wrote, 'Guru Dutt being busy could not pay attention to his own home. His work increased as he became more and more popular.'

Guru Dutt now had a beautiful house, but little time to enjoy it.

Section Fourteen

DESTRUCTION OF A DREAM

1963

'Maine apna ghar tod-taad dala!'

59

DEMOLITION OF A DREAM

'Ever since the bungalow was pulled down, Guru Dutt's home went to pieces gradually.'

—Vasanthi

Geeta had constantly become superstitious about the bad omen the Pali Hill bungalow had brought to her married life. She had conveyed this to Guru Dutt many times. The same bungalow that was the perfect dream home for Dutt not very long ago.

One afternoon Geeta was sleeping in the guest house of the bungalow when at around 4 PM she heard a loud noise. She came out and saw some labourers doing some repair work in the bungalow. But she noticed that they were breaking down the walls of the house. She immediately called up Guru who was in the studio and told him that the labourers were demolishing the house.

'Let them do it! I've asked them to raze it to the ground,' replied Guru Dutt.

Geeta asked, 'But where will we live?'

'We'll live in a hotel. I've already booked a room,' said Dutt.

Guru Dutt had said this so nonchalantly as if it was one of his film sets that was being dismantled after the shooting of the film was completed. After a story was over, captured on celluloid.

This time, it wasn't a film set. It was the dismantling of a dream.

Lalitha says, 'Guru Dutt had agreed to what Geeta wanted but it broke his heart. He used to blame Geeta for the house. Geeta was suspicious and also believed in ghosts.'

The next time writer Bimal Mitra came to Bombay, Guru drove him down to Bungalow No. 48, Pali Hill. The old guard was still there at the gate. As soon as he opened the gate, it seemed as if the opening scene of *Sahib Bibi Aur Ghulam* came out of celluloid and was being played out as reality.

Guru Dutt, like the character of Bhootnath, entered through the gate of what used to be an opulent bungalow. But now there were just ruins. It was as if like Bhoothnath, Guru Dutt too went into a flashback thinking about the old days.

The room where he used to sleep, was now just a pile of bricks overlapping the broken Italian blue marble of his exquisite bathroom. All he could see was splintered timber, chunks of plaster and shattered pieces of a dream.

His thoughts were broken by Mitra's voice. 'Ok, tell me why did you do this to a home built with such love?'

With a sad smile on his lips, he replied,

'Because of Geeta,' Guru said in a low voice.

'What does that even mean?' Mitra asked.

Guru puffed at a cigarette, lost in his thoughts, then blowing smoke he said, 'Ghar na hone ki takleef se ghar hone ki takleef aur bhayankar hoti hai' ('The pain of having a home that you can't call home is worse than the pain of being homeless'). Or perhaps a home that could never become a home.

It was the realisation that the pain of not having a home is better than having a home and realising it could never be a happy home. Profound, yet very painful.

Guru Dutt's mother said, 'Guru's stars were bad. He did not give a second thought to it. The beautiful bungalow was destroyed. Ever since the bungalow was pulled down, Guru Dutt's home went to pieces gradually.'[127]

With Geeta and kids, Dutt shifted to a rented flat in a building called Ashish, opposite Dilip Kumar's bungalow in Pali Hill. The kids thought that they will be returning to their bungalow once the construction work was done. But within a few months Guru and Geeta fought again and realised that their relationship was over and a reconciliation was no more possible.

This time Guru Dutt moved alone to a flat in Ark Royal Apartments on Peddar Road in central Bombay. Geeta Dutt and the three children moved to a rented place near Mehboob Studios in Bandra.

The family was gone. There were no friends around. Only acute loneliness.

In these moments Guru Dutt remembered his old friend, Dev Anand.

Section Fifteen

1964

'Pack up! Pack up!'

60

FINAL DAYS

'I have become an orphan. *Kya karu main*?'

—Guru Dutt to V.K. Murthy

'We were and remained friends till the last, though our meetings started becoming rarer and rarer as we both grew, physically, emotionally and artistically,' said Dev Anand about his old friend Guru.

In his loneliness when there was no one to talk to, Guru Dutt used to call Dev Anand at midnight saying he had a brainwave. Dev remembered,[128] 'He wanted to make another movie with me and I would always tell him, "Come over". He always "came over" and he always discussed his plans…as soon as he set his foot back in the studios, he had another idea and the previous one paled into insignificance. Then I would not hear from him for months at a stretch until he had another brainwave.'

Perhaps Guru Dutt did not plan to make any film with him. He just wanted to go and meet his old friend. Just sit and talk like old times. But he could never share his turmoil even with Dev Anand.

The Madras shooting trips continued. There was no problem of money. He was commanding rupees three lakhs per film as an actor and was most excited about K. Asif's magnum opus *Love and God.* The shooting with Nimmi had began and the industry was abuzz with news that Asif was going to make the film as grand as *Mughal-e-Azam*.

The shooting of his home production, *Baharen Phir Bhi Aayengi*, was going smoothly. He had watched Raj Kapoor's *Sangam* and was very impressed. He wanted to make a colour film. He talked about it with Raj Kapoor and wanted to show him his *Kaagaz Ke Phool.*

Days were spent immersed in work but nights were difficult. It was just loneliness. In Sathya Saran's book *Ten Years with Guru Dutt*, Abrar Alvi talks about a strange conversation he had with Guru Dutt mocking the idea of suicide: 'We used to talk about it. The ways to kill oneself… and we had realised that a man cannot kill himself by swallowing sleeping pills. By the time you can swallow lethal dose, the medicine overpowers you and you conk out.'

And Guru Dutt had replied, 'You must take it like a mother gives medicine to her child…crush the tablets and dissolve them in water.'

Guru Dutt really missed his kids. They would come over during the weekends and those were the happiest moments for him. He doted on his daughter Nina. In April 1964, Guru Dutt went to a hunting trip with his sons Tarun and Arun. Johnny Walker also went with them.

But back in Bombay, the loneliness returned. At home there was only his valet Ratan and cook Ibrahim. His regular conversation companion Abrar Alvi had taken some writing assignments in Madras while cinematographer V.K. Murthy was planning to shift to Bangalore. Guru repeatedly asked them to not leave Bombay. Even offered them to pay the money they had taken as an advance.

Murthy later said,[129] 'Before I shifted to Bangalore, I met him and Abrar Alvi. Guru Dutt told me, "I have become an orphan now. Gharwale nahi hai, tum Bangalore ja rahe ho, Abrar doosra film likne ke liye Madras ja raha hai. (My family is gone, you are going to Bangalore, and Abrar is going to Madras to write a film). I have become an orphan. What do I do?"'

In September 1964, Abrar Alvi came back from Madras and went straight to Guru Dutt's Peddar Road flat. Guru asked him to stay. Abrar said he would come back in a few days. He could feel his sadness but Guru never talked his heart out. 'So many times he would come to the verge of it but then would check himself. He wouldn't let himself be stifled by his own woes; rare were the occassions when he would share them,' said Abrar.[130]

At the midnight of 18 September, an emotionally upset Guru Dutt walked into Abrar's house. He left at five in the morning, wanting to say something all night. But he did not.

Abrar then decided to stay with him for a few days. On 28 September, Abrar shifted to Guru's flat at the Ark Royal Apartments. 'I moved into his Peddar Road flat to write the last few scenes of *Baharen Phir Bhi Aayengi*. For months he had been staying in that big flat alone.'

Lalitha Lajmi had planned a musical evening at her place on 10 October. Ustad Haleem Khan was going to perform a sitar recital. Early October, Lalitha went to invite him but he said, 'Please excuse me. I feel lost in a crowd. I will come later and we will spend time. Then we can have dinner together.' It was to be their last meeting.

On 6 October, Guru Dutt called Dev Anand again. 'In the last days of his life, he called me and said he'd love to have me over. I saw the man then, he'd lost his hair and was weak. He was suffering. He was not the same Guru I'd known. We discussed making a film together. I told him, "Look, why don't you write a great script? Let's do it,"' said Dev Anand.[131]

'He came to the Navketan [Dev Anand's film company] office and said he wanted to come back and make a film there. Dev Anand told him, "Yaar, tumhara ghar hai. Come and make a film soon." Guru smiled and said he wanted Goldie [Vijay Anand] to edit the film. Dev Anand often told us about this last meeting with Guru Dutt,' recalls Amit Khanna.

They made a promise to work together once again, like the promise they had made years ago at Prabhat Studios in Poona during the beginning of their respective journeys.

The same evening Abrar Alvi had moved back to his home.

7 October 1964

A reporter from *The Times of India* visited Guru Dutt Studios where *Baharen Phir Bhi Aayengi* was being shot. Guru was playing a reporter in the movie and wanted to speak with the *TOI* reporter. Guru even asked the reporter if he can visit the newspaper office for research. The visit was planned in the following week.

The scene that was being shot involved Guru Dutt (reporter) and Mala Sinha (newspaper editor). In the scene, he resigns from the job and throws his resignation letter on the table declaring, 'Whether you accept it or not, this is my resignation. I am going.' The editor tries to call him back. But he doesn't return.

Some time ago, K. Asif had shot a grand sequence for *Love and God.* It was shot on a set of caravan serai. In that sequence, Majnu (Guru Dutt) is awakened in the middle of the night by some urchins who tell him that Laila (Nimmi) is waiting for him. He gets up, tip-toes across the room, looks at his father and then disappears into the darkness. He is supposed to fall into a trap laid by those who would deny him love and meet his death.

Laila refuses to believe that her beloved Majnu is dead. She keeps on repeating: 'Majnu cannot die! Majnu cannot die!'

61

THE LAST DAY

FRIDAY, 9 OCTOBER 1964

The shooting of *Baharen Phir Bhi Aayengi* was going on in Guru Dutt Studios. His brothers, Atmaram and Devi Dutt, were shooting for an ad film *Hazrat*. Devi Dutt remembers,[132] 'He asked me to have lunch, suddenly, he decided to pack up and fly kites.' He sent his driver to get his children and together they began flying kites. Much fun was had.

There was nothing that suggested that it would be the last day of Guru Dutt's life.

Guru Dutt, his brother Devi Dutt, Tarun and Arun left the studio together. On the way they stopped at Chiragh Din boutique at Colaba. Guru Dutt loved shopping there. He bought expensive clothes for the children and Devi Dutt. They dropped the kids to their home and Guru asked Devi Dutt to accompany him to his flat. Once at home in the evening, Devi was hungry and Guru Dutt made an omelette for him. They talked cheerfully. 'He gave me two tickets to attend the cricket match the next day.' He didn't have a telephone connection in his flat. They went to the neighbour's house at the ground floor and called Mala Sinha who was shooting in Madras. It was dinner time when he asked Devi to call up Geeta and ask her if she could send the kids to his place. He was missing them.

Geeta reportedly told him that the kids had spent the day with him and now it was too late. She said she would send them the next day. Devi conveyed her message to Guru who had started drinking. 'That was the last meeting I had with my brother,' said Devi Dutt.[133]

As Devi was leaving, Abrar Alvi arrived.

That night Abrar was working on the last scene of *Baharen Phir Bhi Aayengi.* It was about the heroine Mala Sinha who, deserted by her sister and collegues, becomes very lonely. She finally shuts herself up in a mentally deranged state and then dies. Abrar narrated the scene to Guru Dutt. He heard patiently but remained silent. Abrar kept waiting for his reaction but Guru Dutt was silent, lost in his thoughts. Abrar asked, 'Did you like it?'

Guru Dutt replied,[134] 'You know, Abrar, I have a fear that some day I also may go mad. Loneliness could really be oppressive.'

The conversation thread continued. Guru Dutt also told Abrar about a letter he had recieved from a friend who was in a lunatic asylum, recalling that he and Guru knew each other in Poona eighteen years ago. The man had written to Guru after a long time and asked for some money. Guru had observed there was nothing in the letter that suggested that the man was mad.[135]

In this conversation, Guru talked about loneliness and also mentioned how Geeta refused to send her daughter to Guru's place.

Then he heard the scene again. The scene that ended with the heroine's death. In the climax a couplet from the title song (by Kaifi Azmi) is recited:

Badal jaaye agar maali, chaman hota nahi khaali
Baharen phir bhi aati hai, baharen phir bhi aayengi

Guru Dutt finally liked the scene and remarked,[136] 'Our heroine is going to score in this picture.' He was talking about actress Mala Sinha stealing the show with her 'death scene'.

Abrar Alvi kept finalising the scene with Guru's inputs. Around 12.30 at night, Guru went to the neighbour's house and called Raj Kapoor. He asked Raj if he could come and meet him. Raj was surprised but said that it's too late. He promised to come over the next evening. Guru Dutt wanted to discuss the newly formed The Screen Actors' Guild of which he was one of the founder members. But more than that Guru Dutt wanted to show Raj Kapoor his favourite film, *Kaagaz Ke Phool*, and discuss it with him. He could never get over the failure of the film. Guru had sounded sad and lonely.

Guru came back to his flat accompanied by his income tax consultant, Mr Gole. Abrar was still completing the scene. They sat for dinner together but Guru said, 'You two have your dinner. I can't. I am feeling very tired. I would like to retire.'

With these words Guru Dutt went to his bedroom and closed the door.

A restless Geeta Dutt at her mother's apartment at Peddar Road had also retired to bed but couldn't sleep. Around 2 AM she felt extremely uneasy. In the evening they had an argument over the phone as Guru wanted her to send the kids to meet him while she had refused as it was too late. It was nothing unusual. They had had worse altercations in the past.

But the restlessness continued. She felt a strange premonition about something that she couldn't lay her finger on. She wanted to call up Guru but the phone was at a neighbour's house. It was too late to call. She wanted that night to be over soon.

She rang up the neighbours's house the first thing in the morning. Guru's servant came on the line and told her that Guru Dutt was sleeping. Geeta asked him to wake Guru up. The servant went away and came back to say that the door was locked from inside. Geeta asked the servant to break open the door.

At around 3 AM, Guru Dutt came out of the room, woke Ratan up and asked him about Abrar Alvi. Ratan told him that he had left after dinner. Ratan asked if he could make a drink for him. Guru Dutt replied, 'No, just give me the bottle.'

With a bottle of whiskey in his hand, Dutt went back to his room and locked the room from inside.

Guru Dutt never came out of the room alive.

62

JOHNNY! GURU GAYA!

It was 10.30 in the morning of 10 October 1964. It was a Saturday.

Guru Dutt was lying there. Insensate. Finally, his melancholy was over.

There was an unfinished Hindi novel kept by his side and the lights were on. It was as if he had carefully thought about the lighting and composed a frame for a perfect shot for his 'death scene'. He had woven many spells through the poetic glances of his camera and the rebellion in his cinematic language. This was Guru Dutt's last spell. An unusual frame composition for his real departure scene.

Wearing a kurta-pyjama, sprawled on his back, inclined to the right, eyes closed, face relaxed in a serene repose. It was strange but true that he never looked as peaceful in the previous many years as he was looking then. An unusual posture of thoughful, eternal sleep.

His mother recalled, 'I couldn't believe it. How calm and serene was his face! I couldn't believe my son has breathed his last. I went and felt his forehead. It was cold as ice.

Then I went and sat near his feet. I was stunned and sat like a stone.'

Lalitha Lajmi has vivid memories of that morning. She's teary eyed while recounting it, 'He was dead, his right arm out, half-opened eyes, an unfinished book and the right leg folded as if to get up from his bed. There was some coloured liquid in the glass. Dev Anand reached first and sat close to my mother.'

A shocked Dev Anand had cancelled the shoot of *Teen Deviyaan* and was the first one from the industry to reach Guru's Pedder Road flat. 'I was the first man to go into his room. His dead body was lying there. There was a glass of blue liquid on the floor. He was sallow. And dead.'

Abrar Alvi recalled,[137] 'What baffled everyone was the right-hand fore-finger gently resting on his chin—as if he was lost in deep thought.' His leg was lifted as if he was about to get up from the bed. On the side table was a glass with a pink liquid, the sleeping pills *Sonaril* crushed and dissolved in water.[138]

'He's killed himself,' said Abrar as soon as he saw Guru Dutt. Playing in his mind were images from the day when he and Guru had discussed ways to kill oneself. And Guru Dutt had replied, 'You must take it like a mother gives medicine to her child…crush the tablets and dissolve them in water.'

Geeta reached soon and fell unconscious from shock. Their little daughter Nina started wailing, 'Papa, papa get up!' Guru's sister and mother also rushed to the Ark Royal.

Consoling a speechless Geeta, Dev Anand broke down. Holding Guru Dutt's hand, he repeatedly said, 'Guru, uth! Kahan chala gaya tu?' ('Guru, get up. Where have you gone?')[139]

Lalitha recalled, 'The death must have come around 4 or 5 AM. I reached around noon. My mother and husband were already there. Geeta was unconsolable.' With tears in her eyes Geeta said to Lalitha, 'You all will blame me for this. Won't you?'

O.P. Nayyar recalled,[140] 'At around 2 AM the same night that he committed suicide, my wife told me, "Raj Kapoor has phoned for you. He is saying that Guru Dutt is totally inebriated and is crying inconsolably, repeatedly calling for Nayyar Saab!" I was too tired and sleepy to go. I just told my wife to make some excuse. I had an appointment with Guru at his residence anyway the next morning at 10.' Guru kept his word, and Nayyar met his lifeless body the next morning.

Lalitha Lajmi recalls, 'It's a moment frozen for me. The whole film fraternity was there and I was praying for Waheeda to see him for the last time.'

63

THE END

'I know that he had always wished for it, longed for it… and he got it.'

—Waheeda Rehman on Guru Dutt's death

Johnny Walker and Waheeda Rehman were travelling to Madras the day Guru Dutt passed away. Johnny Walker recalled, 'As soon as I entered my room in Hotel Connemera, the telephone rang. It was a trunk call from Bombay, and I was told about the tragedy: "Johnny! Guru gaya!"' Johnny broke down. His friend was gone.

Waheeda Rehman was completely stunned. 'I knew he had tried to commit suicide before, but it was still a terrible shock,' recalled Waheeda who came back to Bombay immediately with Johnny Walker to see Guru Dutt one last time.

'I know that he had always wished for it, longed for it…and he got it,' wrote Waheeda Rehman later on Guru Dutt's death.[141]

O.P. Nayyar, who had a long association with Guru Dutt, was sad and angry, 'True to my straight talking nature, I just blasted those two women for ruining Guru's life—Geeta, right there in front of Guru's dead body in the drawing room and Waheeda at the time of the funeral!'

The sobs and cries filled the house. The smoke of the incense made everything hazy. Guru Dutt was going on his final journey dressed immaculately in a blue suit. His mother could not bear the sight of his last rites being performed. Heartbroken she left for Lalitha's house.

The *Mughal-e-Azam* director, K. Asif, had come to see his friend's face for the last time, 'I won't be able to sleep if I don't see his face.' Guru was playing the lead role in Asif's *Love and God*. Dev Anand, Raj and Shammi Kapoor were requesting the people to stay quiet. Shammi Kapoor helped K. Asif through the crowd and brought him to see Guru Dutt's face for the final time. Asif bent down and lovingly touched Guru Dutt's cheeks and said to Raj Kapoor: 'How innocent he looks…as if he were only asleep.'[142]

Director Shahid Lateef, Johnny Walker's cousin, and two others lifted the bier. Chants of 'Ram naam satya hai', 'Gopal Naam Satya Hai' could be heard. Guru Dutt was on his last journey.[143]

A crying Geeta rushed behind it. Meena Kumari held her. Waheeda Rehman stood there teary eyed with her sister Sayeeda.

It was time to leave. To say the final goodbye.

EPILOGUE

During one of my many conversations with Lalitha Lajmi, the eminent artist who also happened to be Guru Dutt's much loved younger sister, having witnessed his life and times at close quarters, I asked, 'What is the first image that comes to your mind when you think about your brother Guru Dutt?'

She went silent for a few moments, her face acquiring a deeply melancholic look as if traveling back in time.'For years I had dreams of Guru Dutt lying on his bed with his eyes half open and an unfinished book. I try to wake him up. I say, "Get up! get up! your admirers are waiting below the balcony!" I keep looking at his face. He looks like he is in a deep sleep. I keep waiting for him to get up but he is dead. The moment in time is frozen for me forever,' replied a teary-eyed Lalitha.

His wife, Geeta Dutt was shattered and kept on blaming herself for Guru's death. She suffered a nervous breakdown, during which she failed to recognize even her own children or Lalitha. Later, she became a chronic alcoholic and the chances of a career revival also became bleak.

On 20 July 1972, eight years after Guru Dutt passed away, Geeta Dutt died of cirrhosis of the liver. She was 41.

It was a traumatic childhood for the kids Tarun, Arun and Neena. Both the sons wanted to carry forward their parents' legacy. But they could never repeat their father's success. In 1984, they produced the Rekha-Vinod Mehta starrer *Bindiya Chamkegi* (1984) under their father's banner Guru Dutt Films Pvt. Ltd. Directed by Tarun Dutt, the film didn't do well.

They began making another film *Khule-aam*. The action film had Dharmendra-Chunkey Pandey in lead roles. It got stuck and took years to complete.

Tarun Dutt reportedly took his own life in 1989.

Arun Dutt completed the film *Khule-aam* (1992) which was a disaster at the box office. 'The film was completed in 6-7 years and looked dated. He lost a lot of money and Arun never recovered from its failure,' says Lalitha.

The gentle Arun Dutt organized many Guru Dutt retrospectives in India and abroad.

Arun Dutt died on July 2014 by multiple organ failure and cardiac arrest due to prolonged and intense intake of alcohol.

Guru Dutt is survived by his daughter Nina, brother Devi Dutt and sister Lalitha Lajmi.

It has been 56 years to Guru Dutt's death. He was only 39 years of age when he died. He made his brilliant and much-celebrated classics like *Pyaasa, Kaagaz Ke Phool and Sahib Bibi Aur Ghulam* in his early thirties. During the extensive research for this book I realised a strange thing: There is not even a single direct interview of Guru Dutt. The media coverage on him was almost zilch while he was alive. Almost all his contemporaries were in the film magazines in the form of interviews or cover stories, but not Guru Dutt. This despite the fact that he mostly made commercially successful films.

Years after his death, Guru Dutt's cinema began getting immense recognition not just in India but in many parts of Europe. It was as if destiny played out the theme of his immortal *Pyaasa* in real life—the posthumous fame of an artist.

In the late seventies and eighties, a French writer and critic, Henri Micciollo, published a wonderful study of Guru Dutt's cinema. Later, author and filmmaker Nasreen Munni Kabir's detailed work on Guru Dutt's cinema helped immensely in decoding his art. There are many more excellent books written about Guru Dutt's cinema, superb documentaries including interviews of his associates, detailing and applauding his spectacular career. His craft of filmmaking is discussed and studied in many film schools across the world. But most of them do not go into the making and then the unmaking of Guru Dutt, the person. Much has often been said about *Pyaasa* and *Kaagaz Ke Phool* and their semi-autobiographical references.

During the research I realized that events in his personal life that transpired during the shooting of even a shelved film (*Gouri*) found resonance in the scenes of his next film, *Kaagaz Ke Phool*. The line between real and reel kept gradually blurring till it reached a point when the thin line vanished. Where reel became real, with his death. I feel it is very important to recount the story of Guru Dutt in all its three dimensional facets because his cinema was mostly a reflection of his life and times.

Starting from the 1980s many Guru Dutt retrospectives were organized, his films were shown in films festivals across the world. The popularity and the connect that Guru Dutt's films found everywhere proved that their emotions were universal and have not become dated even after decades.

Years ago, this author, as a young boy out of college, had the privilege of watching Guru Dutt's films on big screen at the film club of the India Habitat Centre (New Delhi). The magic I felt remained with me.

Lalitha Lajmi says, 'I was at a screening of *Pyaasa* at the prestigious National Theatre in London. When a young man heard that I am Guru Dutt's sister, he came forward to touch my feet. I had tears in my eyes. How I wish my brother was alive to witness the celebration of his cinema. This baggage from the past and memories are all I have. Time cannot fade these memories.'

FILMOGRAPHY

ACTOR

Picnic		1964
Sanjh Aur Savera	as Dr Shankar Chaudhry	1964
Bahurani	as Raghu Singh	1964
Suhagan	as Vijay Kumar	1964
Bharosa	as Bansi Das	1963
Sautela Bhai	as Gokul	1962
Sahib Bibi Aur Ghulam	as Atulya Chakraborty 'Bhootnath'	1962
Chaudhvin Ka Chand	as Aslam	1960
Kaagaz Ke Phool	as Suresh Sinha	1959
12 O'Clock	as Ajoye Kumar	1958
Pyaasa	as Vijay	1957
Mr. & Mrs. '55	as Preetam Kumar	1955
Aar-Paar	as Kalu	1954
Suhagan		1954
Baaz	as Raj Kumar Ravi	1953
Hum Ek Hain		1946

DIRECTOR

Kaagaz Ke Phool	1959
Pyaasa	1957
Sailaab	1956

Mr. & Mrs. '55	1955
Aar-Paar	1954
Baaz	1953
Jaal	1952
Baazi	1951

PRODUCER

Baharen Phir Bhi Aayengi	1966
Sahib Bibi Aur Ghulam	1962
Chaudhvin Ka Chand	1960
Jawani Ki Hawa	1959
Kaagaz Ke Phool	1959
Pyaasa	1957
C.I.D.	1956
Aar-Paar	1954

NOTES

1. *Conversations with Waheeda Rehman*, Nasreen Munni Kabir, Penguin Viking, 2014.
2. *A Journey Down Melody Lane*, Raju Bharatan, Hay House India, 2010.
3. Interview with the author.
4. 'The last scene', *Filmfare*, May 1966.
5. 'The pain of having a home sometimes can outweigh the pain of not having one.'
6. *My Son Gurudutt*, Vasanthi Padukone, India, serialised in *The Imprint*, April 1979.
7. It is interesting to note that the name 'Gurudutt' was one word. But later, he separated it by a space and made it 'Guru Dutt' which gave the impression that Dutt was his surname. Perhaps as an ode to Bengal where he spent the most beautiful years of his life. Throughout her memoir that was published after Guru Dutt's death, his mother spells Gurudutt as one word.
8. *Unfinished Symphony.*
9. *Unfinished Symphony.*
10. Calcutta left a profound impact on Guru Dutt, and his connection with the city remained integrated in most of his important films. Irrespective of whether the story setting demanded it or not, Bengal made an appearance in his films like a character, consciously or sub-consciously.
11. Earthen lamps.

12. Prayers.
13. Interview with the author.
14. *TIME Magazine*'s All Time 100 Movies List of the greatest films made since 1923 has only three films from India—including Guru Dutt's *Pyaasa*.
15. 'There was a certain nobility about him', Guruswamy, *Screen*, 13 October 1989.
16. *Ten Years with Guru Dutt: Abrar Alvi's Journey*, Sathya Saran, Penguin, 2011.
17. Auspicious prayers and first shot of a new film marking the commencement of its principal photography.
18. https://www.filmfare.com/features/women-were-ready-to-do-anything-for-guru-dutt-devi-dutt-28634-3.html.
19. V.K. Murthy's interview with Patcy N., Rediff.com, 8 October 2004, https://www.rediff.com/movies/2004/oct/08spec1.htm.
20. *Ten Years with Guru Dutt: Abrar Alvi's Journey*, Sathya Saran.
21. *Pyaasa* also had a 'dream song' that remains the only dream song in any Guru Dutt film—the romantic duet: 'Hum aapki aankhon mein'. It was added to the film as an afterthought to provide 'relief' in the midst of a serious story.
22. 'Women were ready to do anything for Guru Dutt: Devi Dutt', Farhana Farook, *Filmfare*, 9 July 2019.
23. *Guru Dutt: A Life in Cinema*, Nasreen Munni Kabir, Oxford University Press, 1997.
24. *Guru Dutt: A Life in Cinema*, Nasreen Munni Kabir.
25. Now in the state of Uttarakhand, India.
26. *Ten Years with Guru Dutt: Abrar Alvi's Journey*, Sathya Saran.
27. Waheeda Rehman interview, Shivendra Singh Dungarpur, *Mint*, 4 May 2013, https://www.livemint.com/Leisure/LUEeD357OifFGP xluE1BgL/Waheeda-Rehman.html.

28. *Binidra*, Bimal Mitra, Mitra & Ghosh Publishers.
29. *Do Bhai* (1947).
30. Guru Dutt's initial films are heavily influenced by the Gyan Mukherjee school of filmmaking.
31. 'Guru Dutt and Geeta had a tempestuous marriage', *Filmfare*, August 2014.
32. 'My friend Guru', Dev Anand, *Open Magazine*, 31 May 2011.
33. Bimal Mitra's *Binidra.*
34. 'Will sound like I am going to supervise a marriage ritual.'
35. 'Qazi Saheb's son has become an actor.' (Films were not considered a very respectable profession then.)
36. 'Here is your scene, your dialogue, this is the shot. If you can do better, go ahead.'
37. 'Both of us technically started at the same time.'
38. 'During those days, one would keep one's word in relationships.'
39. *In Search of Guru Dutt* (1989).
40. *Balraj Sahni*, Balraj Sahni, Hind Pocket Books, 1979.
41. *Romancing with Life*, Dev Anand, Penguin, 2007.
42. *Cinema Modern: The Navketan Story*, Sidharth Bhatia, Harper Collins, 2011.
43. Geeta Roy's family had moved to Santacruz in Bombay.
44. Sandalwood.
45. Bimal Mitra was a renowned Bengali writer who wrote more than one hundred novels and short stories. Many of Bimal Mitra's novels have been made into successful films. One of his most popular works, *Shaheb Bibi Golam* (January 1953) was adapted into a hugely popular movie in Bengal. Guru Dutt later bought the rights of the same novel and made it into one of his most celebrated films in Hindi: *Sahib Bibi Aur Ghulam* (1962). During the making of the film, Guru

Dutt and Geeta Dutt became close to Bimal Mitra and he would stay at their farmhouse during his many extended trips to Bombay. During his stay, Mitra also witnessed many important events in Guru Dutt's life and career during the course of almost two years. Mitra profoundly reflects on Guru Dutt's life and times and Guru–Geeta's relationship in his book *Binidra* (Mitra & Ghosh Publishers).

46. 'Dusky'.
47. 'Don't bore me.'
48. 'Why did Guru Dutt abandon his Bengali directorial debut starring Geeta?', Priyanka Dasgupta, *The Times of India*, 9 July 2018.
49. 'So all you want is for me to look worse than Waheeda Rahman, right?'
50. Bimal Mitra's book.
51. *My Son Gurudutt*, Vasanthi Padukone.
52. https://timesofindia.indiatimes.com/entertainment/bengali/movies/news/why-did-guru-dutt-abandon-his-bengali-directorial-debut-starring-geeta/articleshow/64922979.cms).
53. 'Singing practice.'
54. 'Guru Dutt and Geeta had a tempestuous marriage', Farhana Farook, *Filmfare*, 4 August 2014.
55. *Yours Guru Dutt*, Nasreen Munni Kabir, Lusture Publishers, 2006.
56. 'He was a perfectionist to a fault', R.M. Kumtakar, *Screen*, 13 October 1989.
57. 'The Falcon.'
58. '"Koi door se aawaz de chale aao": Abrar Alvi', *Beete Hue Din*, Shishir Krishna Sharma, 23 March 2020, https://www.cinemaazi.com/feature/koi-door-se-awaz-de-chale-aao-abrar-alvi.

59. 'A Born Artiste', Abrar Alvi, *Outlook*, 31 July 2003.
60. *Filmfare*, August 1953.
61. Abrar Alvi in *Filmfare*, March 1985.
62. 'A Born Artiste', Abrar Alvi.
63. 'What made actor-director Guru Dutt the master of feelings,' Nasreen Munni Kabir, *India Today*, 16 September 2017.
64. *Guru Dutt: A Life in Cinema*, Nasreen Munni Kabir.
65. 'The Artist's First Love', Geeta Dutt, 1958.
66. https://cineplot.com/the-artists-first-love-by-geeta-dutt/.
67. *Filmfare*, June 1963.
68. https://tanqeed.com/my-friend-guru-dev-anand-interview-on-guru-dutt/.
69. *My Son Gurudutt*, Vasanthi Padukone.
70. 'Guru Dutt–O.P. Nayyar: A Rare Tuning', Girija Rajendran, *Screen*, 13 October 1989.
71. 'I am the director, you don't talk to me.'
72. V.K. Murthy's interview with Patcy N., Rediff.com, 8 October 2004.
73. It should be noted that a few years later Guru Dutt's former assistant, Raj Khosla, used the same story and made the very successful film *Woh Kaun Thi?* (1964). There was another film called *Professor* that he had announced when he was making *Pyaasa*. It had Kishore Kumar and Waheeda Rehman in the lead roles. Guru Dutt never made it. But it was later produced by F.C. Mehra in 1962 whith Shammi Kapoor as the hero. It was a huge hit.
74. 'Guru Dutt, the prankster', Sathya Saran, *The Pioneer*, 5 January 2014.
75. 'Women were ready to do anything for Guru Dutt', Devi Dutt by Farhana Farook, 9 July 2019.

76. 'Guru Dutt asked me to show him how cars flew in English films', V.K. Murthy, *The Times of India*, 4 September 2013.
77. V.K. Murthy's interview with Patcy N., Rediff.com, 8 October 2004.
78. *Guru Dutt: A Life in Cinema*, Nasreen Munni Kabir.
79. 'Something must have gone wrong.'
80. Interview with the author.
81. 'Something in him had died.'
82. 'My Friend Guru Dutt', Dev Anand, *Open Magazine*, 31 May 2011.
83. For the BBC documentary *In Search of Guru Dutt* (1989).
84. 'We had grown close when we were working together. I belive the song "Bichhde sabhi baari baari" was also his own story that he couldn't communicate on screen properly.'
85. Nasir Kazi, Johnny Walker's son, in an interview with the author.
86. Based on Sarat Chandra's eponymous novel that has been retold through many adapations in many languages.
87. 'But the things he used to beautifully express through his camera, he was unable to express them himself. What he wanted, he found it very difficult to communicate. His weakness was that he wasn't good at expressing his own feelings.'
88. *In Search of Guru Dutt* (1989), Nasreen Munni Kabir, https://www.youtube.com/watch?v=QJbpT2j7ZBY.
89. 'Nobody really knows what happened on October 10', Raja Sen, 11 October 2004, https://www.rediff.com/movies/2004/oct/11guru.htm.
90. 'It's okay, let's just make a film together.'
91. Ravi's interview, *Screen*, 13 October 1989.
92. Waheeda Rehman interview, Shivendra Singh Dungarpur, *Mint*, 4 May 2013.

93. 'Guruji and I', Waheeda Rehman, *Journal of Film Industry*, 17 November 1967.
94. 'Guruji and I', Waheeda Rehman, *Journal of Film Industry*, 17 November 1967.
95. *Shama*, October 1960.
96. 'O.P. Nayyar: An Intimate Interview', Dr Mandar V. Bichu, *Cinema Sangeet*, http://www.cinemasangeet.com/hindi-film-music/interviews/o-p-nayyar-an-intimate-interview.html.
97. O.P. Nayyar's interview, http://www.opnayyar.org/theman.htm.
98. *Ten Years with Guru Dutt: Abrar Alvi's Journey*, Sathya Saran.
99. 'I feel this way. I wanted to become a director, I became one; I wanted to become an actor, I became one; I wanted to make good films, I made them. I have money, I have everything, yet I have nothing.'
100. V.K. Murthy's interview with Patcy N., Rediff.com, 8 October 2004.
101. 'Hamlet of Films', Abrar Alvi, *Filmfare*, 1964.
102. 'He was a very generous man', Ravi's interview, *Screen*, 13 October 1989.
103. *Binidra*, Bimal Mitra.
104. 'Now I'm so used to it.'
105. 'Nasreen Munni Kabir on Guru Dutt through the eyes of the late Raj Khosla', *DailyO*, 9 July 2015. https://www.dailyo.in/arts/guru-dutt-raj-khosla-nasreen-munni-kabir-pyaasa-kaagaz-ke-phool-in-search-of-guru-dutt-channel-4-uk-baazi-cid/story/1/4860.html.
106. Raj Khosla in *Guru Dutt: A Life in Cinema*, Nasreen Munni Kabir.
107. *Ten Years with Guru Dutt: Abrar Alvi's Journey*, Sathya Saran.
108. Shakila interviewed by Nalini Uchil in 1984, reproduced in cineplot.com, https://cineplot.com/shakila-shakeela-interview/.

109. *Conversations with Waheeda Rehman*, Nasreen Munni Kabir.
110. Bimal Mitra in *Filmy Duniya*, October 1989.
111. Lalitha Lajmi, interview with the author.
112. 'You look like a mouse.'
113. *Sahib Bibi Aur Ghulam: The Original Screenplay*, Dinesh Raheja and Jitendra Kothari, Om Books International, New Delhi, 2012.
114. *Ten Years with Guru Dutt: Abrar Alvi's Journey*, Sathya Saran.
115. Lalitha Lajmi, interview with the author.
116. Lalitha Lajmi, interview with the author.
117. *Ten Years with Guru Dutt: Abrar Alvi's Journey*, Sathya Saran.
118. *Ten Years with Guru Dutt: Abrar Alvi's Journey*, Sathya Saran.
119. 'The more distance you keep between your home and the studio, the happier you'll be. Otherwise, you'll be talking about work at home and about your home in the studio. You'll get confused whether you're coming or going.'
120. *Meena Kumari*, Vinod Mehta, Jaico Publishing House, Bombay, 1972.
121. *Binidra*, Bimal Mitra.
122. *Classics and Cash by Guru Dutt*, *Celluloid* (1963), reprinted by Firoze Rangoonwalla in his monograph *Guru Dutt* (1973).
123. *Yours Guru Dutt: Intimate Letters of a Great Indian Filmmaker*, Nasreen Munni Kabir, Lustre Press, Roli Books, New Delhi, 2006.
124. *Binidra*, Bimal Mitra.
125. *A Journey Down Melody Lane*, Raju Bharatan.
126. Interview with the author.
127. *My Son Gurudutt*, Vasanthi Padukone.
128. 'Tribute to an artist,' Dev Anand, *Screen*, 23 October 1964.
129. 'Guru Dutt was never satisfied with his work', Patcy N., Rediff.com, October 2004.

130. 'Hamlet of Films', Abrar Alvi, *Filmfare*, 1964.
131. 'My Friend Guru Dutt', Dev Anand, *Open Magazine*, 31 May 2011.
132. 'He was my Guru', Devi Dutt, *Screen*, 13 October 1989.
133. 'He was my Guru', Devi Dutt, *Screen*, 13 October 1989.
134. 'Hamlet of Films', Abrar Alvi, *Filmfare*, 1964.
135. 'Khuda, Maut Aur Ghulam,' *Filmfare*, 1964.
136. 'Hamlet of Films', Abrar Alvi, *Filmfare*, 1964.
137. 'Hamlet of Films', Abrar Alvi, *Filmfare*, 1964.
138. *Ten Years with Guru Dutt: Abrar Alvi's Journey*, Sathya Saran.
139. 'How Dev Anand met Guru Dutt', Ranjan Das Gupta, *Mid-Day*, 23 September 2012.
140. O.P. Nayyar interview, http://www.opnayyar.org/theman.htm.
141. 'Guruji and I', Waheeda Rehman, *Journal of Film Industry*, 17 November 1967.
142. 'Aah! Guru Dutt', *Sushma*, October 1964.
143. 'Khuda, Maut Aur Ghulam,' *Filmfare*, 1964.

SELECT BIBLIOGRAPHY

Guru Dutt, 1925-1965: A Monograph, Firoze Rangoonwalla, National Film Archives of India Poona, 1973.

'The Legend of Guru Dutt', Iqbal Masud, *The Illustrated Weekly of India*, November/December 1983.

My Son Guru Dutt, Vasanthi Padukone, serialised in *The Imprint*, 1979.

Guru Dutt: 1925-1964, Henri Micciolo, L'Avant-scène, 1976.

Guru Dutt: A Life in Cinema, Nasreen Munni Kabir, Oxford University Press, 1996.

Asha Bhosle: A Musical Biography, Raju Bharatan, Hay House, 2016.

Binidra, translated in Hindi as *Bichhde Sabhi Baari Baari*, Bimal Mitra, Vani Prakashan, 2010.

Ten Years With Guru Dutt: Abrar Alvi's Journey, Sathya Saran, Penguin, 2008.

A Journey Down Melody Lane, Raju Bharatan, Hay House, 2010.

S.D. Burman: The Prince-musician, Anirudha Bhattacharjee and Balaji Vittal, Tranquebar, 2018.

ACKNOWLEDGEMENTS

Gratitude to all family and friends who always stand by me unconditionally. You know who you are.

The splendid team at Simon and Schuster with a special shout-out to my editor Sayantan Ghosh, Himanjali Sankar and Rahul Srivastava for believing in this story. *Shukriya!*

The seniors in the family: M. Usman, Haseeba Khanam, Shabnam Faridi and Pervez Jamal.

Sahir, Atiya and Irza for their unflinching support, always.

Nazia Erum for everything. For being my first reader, suggesting the most significant change in the narrative of this story and for her love.

And

Myra, who asks why do I write her name in all my books: 'O come on, Papa!'